Power in the Cloud

Innovation at the Intersection of Business and Technology
www.mkpress.com

Power in the Cloud

BUILDING INFORMATION SYSTEMS AT THE EDGE OF CHAOS

Jonathan Sapir

Meghan-Kiffer Press

Tampa, Florida, USA, www.mkpress.com

Innovation at the Intersection of Business and Technology

Publisher's Cataloging-in-Publication Data
Sapir, Jonathan.
Power in the Cloud: Building Information Systems at the Edge of Chaos / Jonathan Sapir, - 1st ed.
   p. cm.
      Includes bibliographic entries, appendices, and index.
      ISBN-10: 0-929652-31-2   ISBN-13: 0-929652-31-2

      1. Management 2. Technological innovation. 3. Diffusion of innovations.
      4. Information technology. 5. Information Society. 7. Organizational change.
      I.Jonathan Sapir. II. Title

HD58.87.S6369 2009   Library of Congress Control Number: 2009929154
658.4'063–dc21   CIP

Published by Meghan-Kiffer Press
310 East Fern Street — Suite G
Tampa, FL 33604 USA

Any product mentioned in this book may be a trademark of its company.

Meghan-Kiffer books are available at special quantity discounts for corporate education and training use. For more information, write Special Sales, Meghan-Kiffer Press, Suite G, 310 East Fern Street, Tampa, Fl, 33604, USA or email info@mkpress.com

MK
Meghan-Kiffer Press
Tampa, Florida, USA
Innovation at the Intersection of Business and Technology
Printed in the United States of America.   SAN 249-7980
MK Printing 10 9 8 7 6 5 4 3 2 1

"In the face of threat, or when galvanized by a compelling opportunity, living things move to toward the edge of chaos. This condition evokes higher levels of mutation and experimentation, and fresh new solutions are likely to be found."

– Richard Pascale, Mark Tillemann, Linda Gioja, *Surfing the Edge of Chaos*

"The attitude that we're shifting into is viewing the world as chaotic. You're never going to understand it. You're never going to control it. Instead, you have to be responsive. You have to make sure that when an opportunity arises you can take advantage of it."

– Danny Hillis, founder of Applied Minds, quoted in *What's Next? Exploring the New Terrain for Business.*

Table of Contents

Preface

This book is part of a larger effort to help companies adopt a revolutionary new way to build information systems for their knowledge workers. Here is how you can access these initiatives.

Visit the Situational Application Resource Center

If you like what you read and want to know more, please visit the PowerInTheCloud web site at www.PowerInTheCloud.com. There you will find lots of information on this topic, provided by both myself and guest writers. There is also a section for each vendor in this market space, which they maintain themselves with the latest information about their products.

Attend a Workshop

Public workshops are held periodically covering all the topics discussed in the book in depth. On-site workshops are also available. Visit www.PowerInTheCloud for more information.

Bring Situational Applications to Your Organization

If you are looking to implement what is described in the book in your organization and you are looking for some advice, let me know by sending me an email at book@powerinthecloud.com. I will help set you on the right path.

Let me know what you think

I always love to hear from readers. If you want to contact me, feel free to email me at book@PowerInTheCloud.com.

Jonathan Sapir
Deerfield, IL
May 2009

Acknowledgements

Before I begin, I would like to thank the many individuals who have helped bring this book to life.

Special thanks to Jeff Kaplan, Jon Pyke, Kevin Smith, Dr. Asaf Adi, Samuel Kallner and Yoav Rubin for contributing their content to the book.

I am grateful to Randall Minter for his insightful comments and detailed reading of the final draft. Randall understands this space better than most, and is well positioned to take advantage of it.

Thanks also to several colleagues for reading the draft and giving me their comments: Glenn Shimkus, Vance Davis, Shannon Topolavich and Mike Bendas.

I particularly want to thank technology marketing and PR consultant Deb McAlister-Holland for the time she spent reviewing the book and pointing out where things were boring or made no sense.

A very loud shout out goes to my phenomenal technical team at SilverTree Systems, both in the USA and in Ukraine. We have worked together for a very long time, and they always get the job done. So tons of thanks to the management team - Eugene Knyazkov, Constantine Kurianoff, Dmitry Minko - and the rest of the gang.

I am enormously indebted to Marty Engel – thanks for hanging in there with me! Thanks also to Barry Moltz for his always insightful advice, and a huge thanks to George Malek who stuck by me when things got rough.

I am grateful to my always supportive wife Joyce for putting up with me through thick and thin, as well as to my three wonderful kids

Jorie, Jake and Jenna, who have had to put up with my warbling while writing.

Finally, I would like to dedicate this book to Vince Sanchez, to whom I will be eternally indebted. Vince went out of his way every work day for an entire year to selflessly help me when I really needed it. Anyone lucky enough to know Vince will be nodding their heads – Vince is the kind of guy you want in your foxhole. Without Vince, there would certainly be no book.

Power in the Cloud

1. Introduction

> *"To see the world ... as a ceaselessly complex and adaptive system requires a revolution. It involves changing the role we imagine for ourselves, from architects of a system we can control and manage to gardeners in a living, shifting ecosystem."* – Joshua Cooper Ramo, *The Age of the Unthinkable*

Information systems in a chaotic world

We live in a chaotic world of increasing and ceaseless change and uncertainty. And it is only going to get worse.

But while it's true that times like these create unprecedented disruption and dislocation, they also create the potential for new power and new fortunes.

The question therefore is: how do we prepare our organizations to not only survive, but to take advantage of the opportunities that rapid change inevitably brings?

This book focuses on the role of information systems in this endeavor. Information systems will become increasingly more critical to the success of every enterprise. How they are built and how they are used should therefore be foremost on the mind of anyone responsible for the well-being of an organization.

This book is a guide to building information systems at the "edge of chaos" – that sweet spot for productive change, where frontline workers have the capability to pursue their own solutions with minimal central control.

The cloud computing revolution

The advent of cloud computing[1] presents an unprecedented opportunity for organizations to revolutionize the way in which they build information systems, and in so doing, transform their business.

For the very first time, everyone who has access to the Internet also has the ability to harness unlimited computing power – much like they can tap into the electrical grid by plugging in an appliance.

As we will see, cloud computing offers many benefits to every organization, large and small. But it offers much more than just lower operational costs and fewer technical resources.

The cloud removes the boundaries imposed by the organizations IT function. All of a sudden, IT is no longer the sole means of delivery (through the enterprise data center) – it also no longer has the sole means of production (through the company's programmers). Now anyone can develop and deploy software solutions at will.

For IT, this is a scary thought, because IT is all about control. IT is a perfect reflection of how we view our organizations – as "well-oiled machines," where ever more knowledge, more efficiency and more hierarchical command and control will produce better results. This paradigm of the organization as a machine is everywhere we look: we need to "jump-start," "shift-gears" and get back "in-sync"; we "re-engineer," and want it all to run "like clockwork"

---

[1] "Cloud computing" in this book refers to the availability of computing power "on demand" – much like electricity is available as needed from the electrical grid. In the same way that a consumer plugs an appliance into a power socket, the user opens a browser and taps into as much computing power as they need, when they need it.

The way we build our information systems reflects this mechanistic view. As a result, we pretend we can predict what will happen in the course of each day, and that we can therefore ascertain what the best course of action for any circumstance that may occur might be. So systems are built to follow the instructions given to them, and only work in the specific conditions programmed for by the engineers. Changes in the environment wreak havoc because these systems have no capacity to adapt.

Cloud computing gives us the ability to adopt a more appropriate approach. And it comes at a time when change is constant – we can no longer simply lay out detailed plans and expect a guaranteed outcome.

A new paradigm: Complex Adaptive Systems Theory

Instead of machines, organizations are increasingly being viewed as living, growing, and ever-changing whole beings – what scientists call a Complex Adaptive System (CAS).[2]

In this world, our role changes from architects of a system we can control and manage, to gardeners in a living, ever-shifting ecosystem.

In this ecosystem, each individual in the organization becomes an active agent in building solutions for their own every day challenges. Since they are closest to the problem or opportunity, they are better able to respond quickly and effectively.

It is a difficult transition for organizations to give up control in this way. But it is the only way to survive in a world that is increasingly uncertain, rapidly changing, and endlessly complex. Complex Adaptive

---

2 *Surfing the Edge of Chaos: The Laws of Nature and the New Laws of Business* – Richard Pascale

Systems are characterized by a high degree of adaptive capacity, giving them resilience in the face of change – exactly what is needed by organizations today.

Organizations that fail to take this step consciously and methodically will not only fail to leverage the considerable benefits it offers – they will have to contend with the anarchy that ensues as employees have no choice but to "do their own thing" to adequately respond to their ever-evolving environment.

To succeed with this approach, you need to understand how and why CAS works. You then need to put the necessary pieces in place to ensure its success in your organization. In this way you can transform your business into a player capable of surviving – and thriving – in an increasingly chaotic world.

Self-service in the cloud

As CAS theory tells us, the speed and efficiency demanded of a resilient and responsive organization can occur only when employees find different ways to make continuous small adjustments that increase profits and decrease costs every day, every week, every month.

The only way to do this is to give them the tools and support they need to serve themselves.

"Self-service" does not mean turning business people into programmers. What it does mean is giving the right set of tools and support to the person closest to the problem, so that they can build powerful software solutions on their own. The goal is to get these knowledge workers to quickly put together "good enough"[3] software solutions to solve specific problems – significantly reducing or even eliminating the time and coordination needed from IT. In this way, it becomes possible to address areas that were previously unaffordable or of low priority to the IT department.

The **target audience** for a self-service approach is an educated professional (e.g., accountant, HR personnel) with modest computer literacy (and interest) that mostly includes the web and MS Office. They have basic computer experience like using a wizard to generate something new; interacting with spreadsheets, documents, and forms; and using drag and drop to rearrange items on the screen.

The **types of applications** being addressed will not replace core business applications. They address a different need – applications that are built for just a handful of users, applications that are used for only a few weeks or months, or applications that address a small piece of functionality. Called "**situational applications**," they are a new software niche, where communities get form-fit, good-enough tools for the very particular needs of the community that uses them.

Situational applications are a potent combination of tools, mindset, and methodology. They provide a formidable force that will help your organization meet today's business challenges quickly and cost-effectively. It will reduce - or even eliminate in some cases - the need to use professional software developers (a valuable resource best used for enterprise-wide solutions), purchase an ill-fitting software package, or kludge a suboptimal, inefficient and incomplete solution using tools like Excel and email.

---

[3] "What is "good enough?" This is discussed in depth in the chapter on the situational mindset.

These **solutions on demand** will help businesses slash expenses and reduce cycle times by more effectively supporting how people work, address challenges and make business decisions. They will allow the business to be more innovative and competitive by supporting new processes more effectively, increasing overall productivity, and facilitating new ways for sharing information.

The ability to do this is being facilitated by the advent of **cloud computing**. Cloud computing for the first time opens up the possibility for businesses to build and deploy powerful systems that don't depend of the resources of the IT department.

How this book is organized

To show how the combination of cloud computing and complex adaptive systems theory can lead to a revolutionary way to build information systems to better meet the demands of our chaotic times, the book look at:

Why?

Why do we need a new approach for building and deploying software solutions?

Why now?

What makes it possible for us to take a new approach at this time?

What?

What are self-service, situational applications? What makes them different from traditional applications?

Where?

Where should you look for places in your organization that would benefit from situational applications?

How?

How do you make the most of a situational approach? What mindset, methodology and tools can significantly improve the productivity of knowledge workers, cut costs and improve competitiveness? What is the best way to implement a situational application environment in your organization? What role should IT play in supporting situational applications?

What to do next

How do you get started?

Who this book is for

This book is not technical. It is aimed at those people in the organization who can get the most out of situational applications:

- **Executive Management.** How will situational applications reduce time to market for new solutions, improve the organizations overall productivity, and increase return on IT investment?

- **Departmental Managers.** How will situational applications help me improve my department's productivity and effectiveness?

- **Business Professionals.** How will situational applications provide me with better tools to do my job more effectively?

- **IT Management.** How will situational applications reduce the amount of effort and risk required to build solutions, and how will they allow me to service my user base more effectively?

- **Business consultants.** How will situational applications help me improve my clients organizations, and allow me to expand my service offerings?

- **Systems Integrators.** How can I take advantage of situational applications to help my clients and increase my revenue?

2. Why we need a new approach

"The health, competitive power, and even survival of an enterprise largely depends on its ability to understand and harness the power of knowledge workers who are enabled to take responsibility for providing automatic solutions to meet many of their business needs." – SOA meets situational applications: Examples and lessons learned, IBM System Journal, July 2008

Let's start by taking a look at the need to change.

In this chapter, we will look at:

- why knowledge workers have become the most fertile area for improving company performance;

- why the unique world of the knowledge worker requires a very different type of information systems than we have built in the past;

- why the new generation of knowledge workers will insist on a new approach;

- why the speed of change requires us to take a very different approach to building information systems than our current methodologies allow for;

- why the holes we have in our information access causes so much (hidden) wasted time; and

- why it is not feasible for IT alone to address these needs.

The growing value of knowledge workers

"An important scientific innovation rarely makes its way by gradually winning over and converting its opponents.... What does happen is that its opponents gradually die out and that the growing generation is familiarized with the idea from the beginning."—Max Planck, The Philosophy of Physics, 1936

Knowledge workers now make up the majority of both the operating expense and the competitive advantage of most organizations. Knowledge workers are also the area where organizations most often realize competitive differentiation—where they design products, support and retain customers and partners, minimize risk, and maximize profit. Their productivity is quickly becoming the key factor in determining profitability in today's economy.

The productivity of knowledge workers is not just a *Fortune 500* business problem. Small companies need better ways to manage knowledge workers even more, because they have to be even more flexible, more responsive, and more "right" (that is, make better decisions) — even small mistakes can be fatal to them.

The value of the knowledge workers will continue to grow as a result of factors such as:

- The **growing need to reduce costs** at a time when increasing revenues is hard to do. The middle-office, the primary home of knowledge workers, is a fertile area to try to reap efficiencies— back-end systems like ERP only directly touch a fraction of employees in the organization and of those employees they do touch, they only touch them a fraction of the time. The **increasing ratio of nonstandard to standard tasks**. Problems that can be completely standardized are either being fully automated, removing the human from the loop, or, through the use of self- service technologies, are being delegated to users outside the organization. Take, for example, checking in at the airport. Before the advent of self- check-in, service representatives were needed to handle all check-ins, most of which were standard and required relatively little knowledge. Only exceptional cases needed to be handled by supervisors or "experts." Now, all standard check-ins are automated and only the exceptions remain, thereby eliminating the need for low-knowledge service representatives. To be successful, these workers need the right tools to meet the unique needs of customers and situations that might arise.

- The **increasing role of knowledge workers in evaluating net worth**. When Peter Drucker proclaimed the age of the knowledge worker, he predicted that competition in business would be all about the management of knowledge resources. The tangible value of knowledge workers is apparent in evaluating the net worth of an organization, where knowledge and related intangibles now account for the overwhelming proportion of the average corporation's perceived worth.

- The **potential revenue from selling "virtual knowledge packets."** The advent of new technology provides organizations with an unprecedented opportunity to package and sell their knowledge. It is the next logical step, and it will lead to the significant increase in the value of knowledge workers.

- The **increasing amount of information** that needs to be dealt with on a day-to-day basis, including the growing complexity of rules and regulations that need to be adhered to in the complex global world.

- The **increasing dispersion of the workforce across time and space** makes the smooth transition of work from one employee to the other increasingly difficult to manage and control, and increases the potential lag time between events happening and the relevant people/systems being aware of them so they can take the necessary action. Much looser organizational structures require technologies that support virtual teams of specialists scattered around the globe who can collaborate independent of location, time zone, technology, or language. These technologies must also support the instant reconfiguration of such teams. Teams that are formed quickly must be able to define their work environment and address many of their own needs as they arise.

The complex world of knowledge workers

> Knowledge workers are the last remaining bastion of untapped productivity.

The productivity and effectiveness of knowledge workers are increasingly critical factors in determining the fate of the 21st century organization. But their world is quite different from the world that IT has supported in the past, and a new approach is needed to make these workers succeed.

These solutions need to take into account the different world of the knowledge worker:

- **The knowledge worker's environment is dynamic and unpredictable**. Their actions and decisions are often driven by unexpected events and exceptions to documented business processes. They have to deal with the growing amount of information and the growing complexity of relationships and regulations in the global economy. To succeed, knowledge workers have to respond instantly to continuous changes, often relying on their know-how, personal relationships, and unique understanding of their environment. This tacit knowledge is not easy articulated or codified.

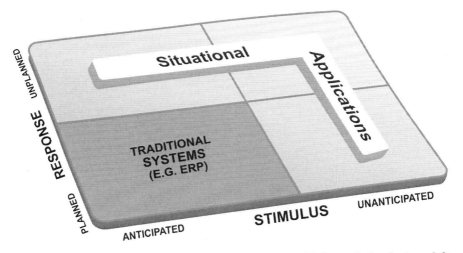

Figure 1: The knowledge worker lives in a world beyond the bottom left quadrant, buffeted by unanticipated events requiring unplanned responses. Address the three quadrants outside of standard, rigid transaction-based systems that respond to anticipated business stimuli requires something far more flexible and dynamic than the solutions available to date.

Today, employees address these quadrants with a combination of email, spreadsheets, and word processing tools to help them coordinate their work and maintain focus on the tasks at hand.

- **Knowledge workers need the ability to approach their activities in the way they feel most comfortable.** Knowledge workers have individual learning and communications styles; "one- size-fits-all" is not appropriate.

27

- **Knowledge workers need to respond quickly to constant change**. The world of the knowledge worker is always in flux. Therefore, in order to effectively adapt, they need to be able to do things like modify rules without waiting for IT to take action.

- **Knowledge workers get overlooked** because the cost of automating most knowledge worker-related processes is far greater than the expected savings or productivity gains (using traditional methods). Because specialized applications are so expensive to develop and maintain, only the most critical and expensive processes tend to be tackled—payroll, sales order processing, etc.

- **The knowledge workers world is not easily accessible to outsiders**. Many knowledge workers would argue that there is no common structure and flow to their work. Since their work is more variable and unpredictable than production or administrative work, if you want to understand it, you have to look long and hard. Much of what they do is invisible—it takes place inside the human brain.

- **Knowledge workers don't like to be told what to do**. Knowledge workers are like artists. They want (and usually need) creativity and variation in their work, and often resent attempts to "streamline" or automate their work in any way—especially when imposed from the outside. The belief that processes can be imposed on knowledge workers is particularly far-fetched.

- **The knowledge workers world is full of exceptions**. In back-end systems, like accounting, exceptions should be extremely rare, and can therefore be dealt with manually, with relative ease. For front-end systems like ATM transactions, again, strict procedures are crucial for success. The whole idea of these systems is that they can be totally automated. In the world of the knowledge worker, things are much more messy. People like to tinker, to change things. People are unpredictable. Exceptions are a way of life and too numerous to be planned for in advance. This is a world very much disconnected from the world of transaction-based systems.

The changing workforce

> *"How ya gonna keep 'em down on the farm after they've seen Paree?"* – song by Young, Lewis, and Donaldson

When computers were first introduced into the workplace, they were viewed as mysterious and intimidating by many business users. Those users learned the functionality by rote, and never strayed from what they'd been taught.

The way we build information systems today still assumes a workforce that is computer illiterate. Users must be provided with everything they need and are given little ability to create their own solutions (other than standalone, desktop applications for their private use).

But this assumption no longer applies. Not only are we seeing a very new type of worker, one that is much more computer literate, but even the older workforce is becoming more IT savvy and capable of more than we give them credit for.

But it's even more than that. The Millennials flooding the workforce have different expectations, skills, and values. After all, they are the first generation to grow up with IT as an inseparable part of their environment.

Their characteristics include the following:

- Because they are used to **customizing and individualizing** everything—from phone ring tones to their Facebook pages - when they move into a workplace, they translate these experiences into wanting to select their own tools, customize their environment, and take responsibility for automating as many activities as possible.

- They tend to be highly **creative, collaborative, and have little or no patience** for established lines of authority. They won't want to wait for IT to get to the bottom of the application development priority stack. For this generation, a situational approach to building systems will seem natural. Many will

> *"This generation [Millennials] is exceptionally curious, self-reliant, contrarian, smart, focused, able to adapt, high in self-esteem, and globally oriented. These attributes combined with [Millennials] ease with digital tools spell trouble for the traditional enterprise and the traditional manager. This generation will create huge pressures for radical changes in existing companies."*
>
> —Don Tapscott,
> Growing up Digital

have gone through programming classes in high school (and even junior high) and college. They know what can be done, and they are not going to know what the big deal is to write a system to meet the needs of their job. With the right tools, they can do it themselves.

- They **live and breathe innovation**, constantly looking for ways to do things better and therefore expect constant change. Unafraid of the technology, they are constantly trying to push it to the next level.

- They are **the ultimate "now" generation**. The interactivity and speed of the Internet have greatly increased the process of communicating. This generation views the world as 24/7 and demands real-time and fast processing—the idea of waiting weeks (or even hours) for a response is just not in their worldview.

Millennials will automate their work themselves whether management likes it or not. Therefore, it is much better to facilitate these efforts than sweeping them under the carpet. It is an opportunity—it should be used.

By the same token, those companies that force its employees to go through IT to get systems built are not going to get the best and the brightest. The reverse will be true—providing an environment that the younger members of the workforce can thrive in will attract the right kind of employees.

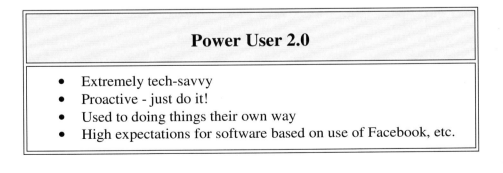

Power User 2.0

- Extremely tech-savvy
- Proactive - just do it!
- Used to doing things their own way
- High expectations for software based on use of Facebook, etc.

- Nintendo logic – willing to engage in trial and error
- Expects instant results
- Expects an entertaining, dynamic user experience
- Expects software to be highly customizable to their exact needs

The need for speed

"When change within your organization is slower than that without, you're in real trouble. We can't predict the future, but we can learn to react a lot faster than our adversaries." - Jack Welch, ex-CEO, GE

The challenges faced by knowledge workers is compounded by the relentless, endless compression of "float" - the time between what was and what is to be, between past and future.

Not too long ago, a check would take a couple of weeks to find its way through the banking system. This "float" was used by many to their advantage. Today, of course, money can move through the system instantaneously, and this has resulted in significant impacts on the world of finance. Similarly, we have witnessed the disappearance of information float. In the past, it took significant amounts of time for information to travel. It took centuries for information about the smelting of ore to cross a single continent and bring about the Iron Age; during the time of sailing ships, it took years for that which was known to become that which was shared; it took decades for the steam engine and automobile to attain universal acceptance. It took years, too, for radio and television to become pervasive. Today, countless devices utilizing microchips leap virtually overnight into universal use throughout the world.

Organizational responsiveness and effectiveness are increasingly moving targets. No situation or challenge is the same as the last one. To be effective now and in the future, organizations must be able to adapt existing ways of working to new challenges with speed and agility that was unimaginable even two years ago. Technology needs to allow companies to act appropriately and competitively regardless of the situation—without long lead times or high incremental expense.

The need for continuous improvement and innovation

> *"The days of market stability and competitive advantage from a single innovation are over. Today, companies must respond to new entrants in their industries that come from nowhere. And they must not just innovate, they must set the pace of innovation, gaining temporary advantage, one innovation at a time, and then move on to the next."* – Peter Fingar, Extreme Competition

Kaizen (Japanese for "improvement") is a Japanese philosophy that focuses on continuous improvement throughout all aspects of life. When applied to the workplace, Kaizen activities continually improve all functions of a business, from manufacturing to management and from the CEO to the assembly line workers.

Kaizen is a daily activity, the purpose of which goes beyond simple productivity improvement. It is also a process that eliminates overly hard work, teaches people how to perform experiments on their work, and how to learn to spot and eliminate waste in business processes.

People at all levels of an organization can participate in kaizen, from the CEO down, as well as external stakeholders when applicable. The format for kaizen can be individual, suggestion system, small group, or large group. It is usually a local improvement and involves a small group in improving their own work environment and productivity. This group is often guided through the kaizen process by a line supervisor; sometimes this is the line supervisor's key role. (This role will be played by a Situational Application Analyst as described later in the book).

While kaizen usually delivers small improvements, the culture of continual aligned small improvements and standardization yields large results in the form of compound productivity improvement.

Situational applications can perform the role of kaizen for knowledge workers by allowing them to make continual changes in their work using software.

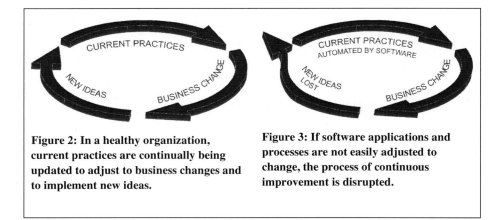

Figure 2: In a healthy organization, current practices are continually being updated to adjust to business changes and to implement new ideas.

Figure 3: If software applications and processes are not easily adjusted to change, the process of continuous improvement is disrupted.

But while the ability to sense and respond to market change is critical, it is not enough. The ability to also anticipate customer needs, and shape markets, will become the core competencies for successful companies, large and small.

What's new is that it is no longer simply a question of coming up with clever new products. Now, the ability to innovate with services wrapped around those products becomes critical. A large-scale example of this is a service like OnStar, which allows a car company to sell you not just a car, but an ongoing service that provides "peace of mind on the road."

There is a need to go beyond just delivering products or services by offering unprecedented convenience and affordability to customers, and even, as Starbucks has taught us, delivering experiences that command a premium.

And there is a need to do it continuously. As Peter Fingar has pointed out:

> "The whole notion of being able to set the pace of innovation in your industry becomes a radical thing that you have to be able to do, otherwise you immediately get commoditized."

Situational applications offer the kind of self-service, continuous trial-and-error experimentation that is necessary in order to discover what works and what doesn't in a manner that is low cost and fast.

The high cost of not finding information[4]

Having the right information at the right time – and *understanding where it came from and the context in which it was created* – is more critical than ever. The most extreme example of this of course is NASA's Mars Climate Orbiter spacecraft, which just disappeared one day after flying nine-and-a-half months and 416 million miles flawlessly. It turns out that unbeknownst to the metric-based NASA, its contractor had submitted acceleration data in pounds of force instead of the metric equivalent, newtons. By not converting the pounds to the metric measurement, the spacecraft was lost.

Everything from market analyses through product design through decisions to invade other countries – all these things are based on having the right information available. The very complexity of the decisions we make and the products we manufacture makes it impossible to check, test and retest them adequately enough to be sure that they will function properly in any circumstance. Information disasters are a growing threat, and one that few businesses can ignore.

Information holes

There is a wide range of information holes that we need to deal with:

Lack of context

Information disasters are caused not necessarily by the lack of information, but rather by not connecting the right information to the

---

[4] Susan Feldman,
www.kmworld.com/Articles/ReadArticle.aspx?ArticleID=9534

right people at the right time. People use information within the context of what they are doing. They need to have access to the right information, but only when they need it. And they need to be assured that the access is guaranteed, easy, fast and reliable.

Wrong information

Decisions are made based on the wrong information being available. For example, a support person denies a client assistance because the information they have tells them the client has not paid for their support contract.

Missing or incomplete information

It's not just the information itself that is vital to the organization. How the information is exchanged and tracked is important, so that when people disappear, the reasons why decisions were made remain behind.

Too much information

In the extreme case of the Three Mile Island Nuclear Power Plant disaster, for instance, operators had so many error messages thrown at them that they couldn't identify the main cause of the problem.

Scattered information

The information needed is in multiple repositories and databases all over most organizations. No one knows what exists or where it is, and there is no single unified access point to it.

Information overload

We are bombarded by e-mail, copies of presentations, alerts of new interesting articles, meetings and all of the other information trappings that go with being a knowledge worker. We spend hours trying to track down something that we found only yesterday, but it seems to have disappeared.

The costs of not finding information

So we spend a lot of time spinning our wheels looking for things and not finding them. This leads to:

Bad decision making

There really is no metric we can use to compare the value of a good decision to a bad one. How do we know that a project has taken twice as long as it should have for lack of access to information? The fact is that knowledge workers rarely turn out measurable products, and each project is slightly different from the one before. If they can't find the information on which to base their output, they may have to submit poor quality work to meet a deadline.

Employee burnout

Employee burnout rate may be higher because job satisfaction is low when workers spend their days unsuccessfully searching and reworking information.

Recreating information that already exists

Recent research on knowledge work shows that knowledge workers spend more time recreating existing information than they do turning out information that does not already exist.

Wasted time looking for information

Knowledge workers spend from 15% to 35% of their time searching for information; they are successful in finding what they seek

50% of the time or less; and 40% of corporate users reported that they cannot find the information they need to do their jobs on their intranets.

Lost revenue

There is the potential cost of lost revenue if customers can't find the products they want to buy, and increased call center and online technical support costs because they can't find the answers they need. This is exacerbated when calls are escalated to another person rather than being answered immediately.

Lost creativity and innovation

What we can't do is measure the increase in creativity and original thinking that might be unleashed if knowledge workers had more time to think and were not frustrated with floundering around looking for information.

ITs application backlog and the long tail

The long tail

The concept of the "long tail" originates from an article by Chris Anderson in *Wired Magazine*[5] in which he described the niche strategy of certain businesses such as Amazon.com or Netflix. The Long Tail is the 80% of stuff that didn't used to be worth selling, but now is worth selling because the technology is there to make it profitable.

In practical terms, this means that many individual low-value items can add up to create significant value. For example, a store like Wal-

---

[5] http://www.wired.com/wired/archive/12.10/tail.html

Mart has physical limitations. Shelf space in Wal-Mart stores is expensive and scarce – it doesn't have room to sell a little bit of everything, so it stocks carefully selected items and makes all of its money selling many copies of these things. In contrast, virtual stores such as Amazon and Netflix profit from the long tail—they don't have any shelf space limitation and succeed by selling just a few copies of many different things. In fact, according to Anderson, Amazon makes 25 percent of its sales, and an even higher percentage of its profits, selling inventory that is not on any retail shelf anywhere.

Applying that concept to applications results in a graph (see below) that shows strategic applications at the top with a long tail at the bottom consisting of situational applications. The level of customization required for the IT department to build small applications for individuals made those applications far too expensive and labor intensive.

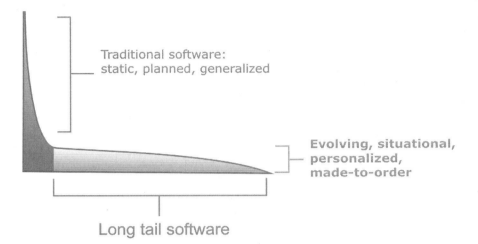

Figure 4: There is a long tail of applications that should be developed but can't be, because the startup and deployment of building them is too high for the perceived value. By lowering these costs, we can make the long tail more feasible.

But the whole purpose of software in business is to support the way an organization does business – from the way a business runs its hiring and firing to the way it orders materials to the way it tracks sales. And while some of these are relatively common in name from business to business (recruiting, for example), in practice, they are usually highly customized.[6] There is therefore a very long tail of software applications that could be built.

However, because long tail applications have small audiences and limited relevance horizons, they tend not to make economic sense given the given way IT is. The startup costs alone make building these applications prohibitive. By lowering the bar relative to the cost of developing such applications, these applications become much more viable.

---

[6] *The long tail of software. Millions of Markets of Dozens* – Joe Kraus. http://bnoopy.typepad.com/bnoopy/2005/03/the_long_tail_o.html

By themselves, these low-complexity applications don't compare in ROI to these core applications. But many individual low-value items can add up to create significant value. So while these applications may not individually be cost-effective for IT to implement, in the aggregate they represent serious money in terms of unrecognized cost savings, inefficient operations, and unrealized business opportunities.

It is these small adjustments that are going to make the difference between success and failure in a constantly changing world. Therefore, there needs to be a way to effectively address the long tail.

3. Foundations for a new approach

"The shift to cloud computing will dramatically reduce the cost of information technology, but let's be clear — the implications of this particular shift go far beyond cost savings." – Shane Robison, EVP, HP - The Next Wave: Everything as a Service

To effectively address all the challenges raised in the previous chapter, a radical change is needed. There are two key factors facilitating this change:

- A new **means** of getting things done: Cloud computing, which dramatically reduces the complexity and time needed to go from idea to realization, and is available to everyone.

- A new **way** of thinking to take advantage of the new means available: Shifting from thinking of the organization as a machine to thinking of it as a living organism.

Cloud computing

"If something is a good idea, it's going to happen. And so, you can fight it, or you can do it." –
Jeff Bezos, Amazon CEO

What is cloud computing?

Wikipedia defines cloud computing as follows:

*The **cloud** is a metaphor for the Internet, based on how it is depicted in computer network diagrams, and is an abstraction for the complex infrastructure it conceals. It is a style of computing in which IT-related* *capabilities are provided "as a service," allowing users to access technology-enabled services from the Internet ("in the cloud") without knowledge of, expertise with, or control over the technology infrastructure that supports them.*

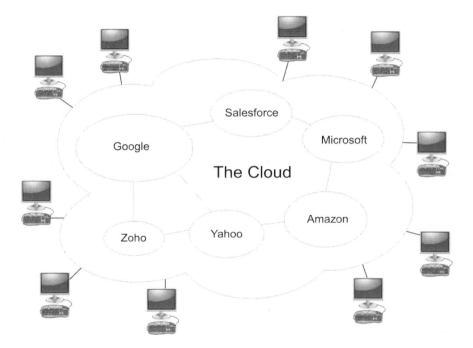

Figure 5: The term cloud is used as a metaphor for the Internet, based on how the Internet is depicted in computer network diagrams, and is an abstraction for the complex infrastructure it conceals.

The ultimate goal of cloud computing

The best thing about cloud computing is that by migrating your business to the cloud you get a world free of worry about things that have nothing to do with your core business.

With cloud computing, companies can run every information system they rely on without owning any tech equipment. The ultimate goal of cloud computing for a SMB is to become a serverless enterprise.

Cloud computing lets businesses rent access to applications and IT infrastructure that reside on the Internet, pay for them on a subscription or per-use basis and provide employees with access to information from anywhere at any time with nothing more than a connected device. No more hassling with software updates or growing storage requirements. No more expanding data centers to make room for additional racks of servers to support a growing business. Maintenance, scalability, performance, backup, disaster recovery – all gone.

With cloud computing, you outsource the functions that don't make you special to someone who specializes in them.

How it works

Think of it this way - what if you had to concern yourself with providing the electricity needed to run your business? If there was no outlet to plug your lights and machines into, you would have to go look for a generator, buy it, implement it, hire engineers to keep it running, make sure you have backup, and make plans for any disaster recovery that might befall such a critical component of your business.

Plug into the cloud

It used to be this way, in the days before the electric grid, and being able to produce your own electricity was a huge competitive advantage. But once the grid was in place, it quickly became a major liability. Companies that moved to the grid significantly reduced their costs, and they could focus on their business. In addition, having access to cheap, unlimited electricity meant they could afford to make use of electrical components that before may have been cost prohibitive.

There is a very strong parallel between this and IT. Harvard professor Nicholas Carr has written a book about this called The Big Switch. In the same way that companies moved to the electrical grid, so they will move to the computing grid in the "cloud." Just like plugging your device into an outlet to get electrical power, you point your browser to the appropriate application in the cloud to get the service you need.

Say goodbye to servers

There are enormous advantages to be had. You never have to buy servers again. You never have to worry about backups and disaster recovery. You never need to hire networking specialists to keep your infrastructure running. You never have to patch and upgrade your hardware or software.

Say hello to a new world of powerful applications

But it's even more than that. Once you are plugged into the cloud, you have access to thousands of new applications that can help your business, many of them free or low cost. Anyone anywhere in the world, at any time - employees, partners, clients - needs only a browser to access your organizations information. No more downloads, installs, updates.

Simpler integration

Unlike the costly and complex way in which integration among disparate systems takes place now, applications in the cloud are standards based and much more open than traditional applications. This paves the way for building powerful composite solutions that pull data and use functionality from multiple applications, and significantly expands the type and sophistication of applications that can be developed by non-programmers.

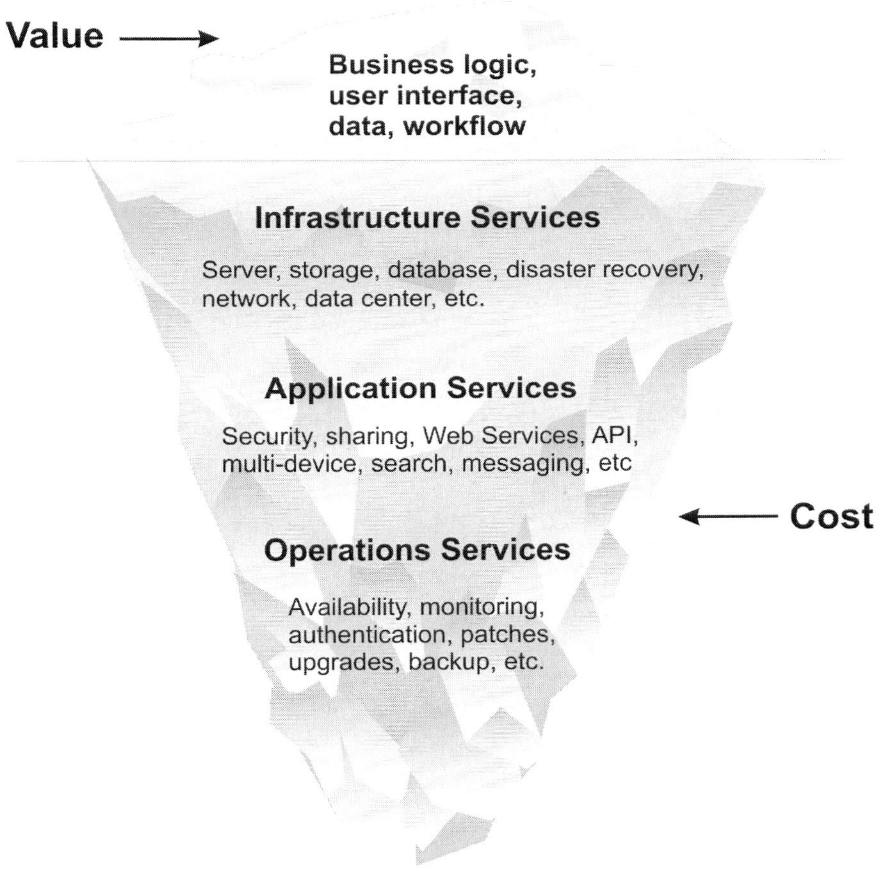

Value ⟶

**Business logic,
user interface,
data, workflow**

Infrastructure Services

Server, storage, database, disaster recovery,
network, data center, etc.

Application Services

Security, sharing, Web Services, API,
multi-device, search, messaging, etc

⟵ **Cost**

Operations Services

Availability, monitoring,
authentication, patches,
upgrades, backup, etc.

Figure 6: An application is the tip of the iceberg. All the underlying costs required to support the application are essentially "below the surface." Cloud computing eliminates these costs, leaving just the value.

Complex Adaptive Systems Theory

"The big payoff of the living systems point of view is that what is remote and unnatural within the traditional frame of reference becomes sensible and accessible within the complexity mindset." - Richard Pascale, Mark Tillemann, Linda Gioja, *Surfing the Edge of Chaos*

Paradigms are important because they determine not only how we understand things, but also the way in which we deal with them. If your worldview included the belief that the Earth was flat, it would be highly unlikely you would set off on an ocean voyage for fear of falling off the edge. Paradigms help us make sense of the world. And they help determine how we approach building information systems.

There has been a recent shift in thinking[7] about how organizations work, and with this shift will come a very different approach to building information systems. Let's take a look at where we are and where we are heading.

---

[7] See *Business Agility: Sustainable Prosperity in a Relentlessly Competitive World* – Michael Hugos.

A Clockwork Universe

"The robustness and endurance of the machine as the predominant metaphor of 20th century management practice is nothing short of amazing given the mounting evidence that it simply doesn't work." – John Hagel, Out of the box

Most of our deepest beliefs and assumptions are grounded in a mechanistic view of the world that was adopted in the early days of the Industrial Revolution, dating back to Rene Descartes, the 17th-century French mathematician and philosopher who believed humanity inhabited a "clockwork universe." Based on these ideas, Isaac Newton articulated a view of the world that imagined the cosmos to be a gigantic clock-like mechanism composed of separate parts acting upon one another with precise, linear laws of cause and effect.

This perspective has led to the belief that with ever more knowledge, more efficiency, and more hierarchical command and control, we could pull a lever at one place and get a precise result at another, and know with certainty which lever to pull for which result. So, for centuries, we have been designing and pulling those levers, all the while hammering people to behave in the compliant, subordinate manner one expects from a well-trained horse. Rarely have we gotten the expected result.[10]

This image of ourselves as operators of this enormous machine has remained unquestioned until relatively recently. It continues to haunt the way we try to improve efficiency in our organizations—consider the concept of "re-engineering." The term alone, says John Hagel, "attests to the depth to which mechanistic thinking has become embedded in our corporate psyches." Since the goal was to make the organization run like a "well-oiled machine," when it didn't, it meant looking for another solution to impose on the organization – reflected in the terminology, like "jump-start," "shift gears," and "out-of-sync."

> We want things to work like clockwork, but they rarely do. Instead of trying to force the clock to work better, we need a more realistic way of looking at the way things really work.

The influence of Newton is deeply felt in IT. If we get those specifications right, everything will work like, well, clockwork.

But an awful lot has changed since the 1600s. Our world is not Newton's world. 17th-century concepts don't work for us in the twenty-first century. Newton's laws were simple, neat, and described a world that could ultimately be controlled. Unfortunately, it doesn't work. Until this obsolete, mechanistic worldview is abandoned, we will not effectively address the needs of the organization.

Complex Adaptive Systems

More than sixty years ago, scientists knew that Newton was wrong about the way the world worked. It turns out that we do not live in an even remotely linear world; in fact, our world should be categorized as nonlinear. But despite the fact that the machine metaphor has been all but abandoned by 20th-century science, IT continues to clutch the reassuring image of the clockwork organization. We have to come to grips with the fact that we are not cogs in a timepiece, but integral participants in a distinctly living, growing, and ever-changing whole being – what scientist call a *complex adaptive system.*

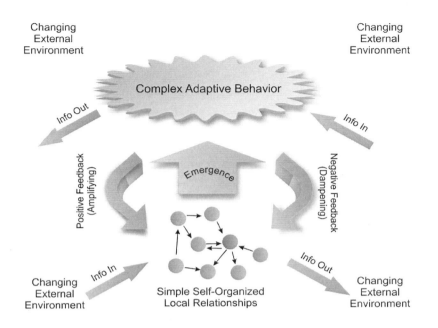

Figure 7: In a Complex Adaptive System, patterns "emerge" from the self-organized behavior of semi-autonomous agents reacting to changes in their environment.

A complex[8] adaptive system (CAS) is a system of semi-autonomous agents who have the freedom to act according to a set of simple rules in order to maximize a specific goal. A CAS is highly adaptive, self-organizing, interrelated, interdependent, interconnected entity that behaves as a unified whole. It learns from experience and adjusts (not just reacts) to changes in the environment.

Complex adaptive systems are all around us: the weather, ant colonies, the stock market, our immune systems, neighborhoods,

---

[8] Note that "complex" does not mean "complicated." A mechanical clock is complicated in that is composed of many parts that work together in a special way. But it does not exhibit the "complex" behaviors that are described by CAS.

governments, porting events, and, most important, the organizations in which we work. The "participants" in every system exist and behave in total ignorance of the concept but that does not impede their contribution to the system. And every individual agent of a CA is itself a CAS: a tree for example is a CAS within a larger CAS (a forest) which is a CAS in a still larger CAS (an ecosystem).

This theory can be demonstrated by what happens when a set of traffic lights at a busy junction cease to function. At first, there is a lot of hesitancy, but gradually, a pattern emerges which the motorists recognize and they all start to cross a few at a time in each direction; and very often, what emerges is more effective than the normal pattern. This continues very well until in a complex world a cop arrives and starts to direct the traffic, and of course the queues build up and are worse than usual. The system is clearly quite complex as there are no set rules, but more importantly, it is adaptive in that the pattern changes as the circumstances change—hence a complex adaptive system.

Properties of a Complex Adaptive System

While the Newtonian machine was a metaphor, the organization as a living organism in not a metaphor—the organization *is* a living organism, whether we want it to be or not. Viewing it as such will open up new insights in how to build better information systems. Here are some examples.

- It is accepted that it is impossible to fully understand and anticipate everything.

- A system that is rigid isn't capable of rapidly responding to a changing environment, and will eventually die. In addition, nothing novel can be expected from systems that have high degrees of order and stability. On the other hand, a system in chaos is too formless to coalesce, and cease to function as a system. The most productive state to be in is at the" edge of chaos" where there is maximum variety and creativity, leading to new possibilities[9].

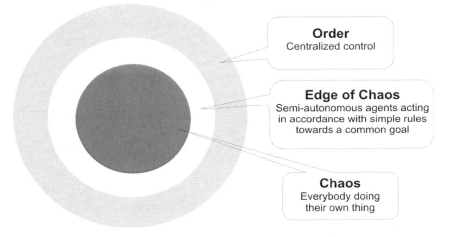

Figure 8: The Edge of Chaos. Systems need to balance between chaos and order to survive and adapt.

- There is a tenuous connection between cause-and-effects. Small changes can have huge effects. Alternatively, large changes may have little effect. Attempts to direct result in unintended consequences - the belief that more sophisticated systems will result in greater efficiency can have the opposite effect.

- While it often appears that the agents in a system interact in apparently random ways, patterns emerge - as we saw in the traffic example. We see this all over nature—for example, a termite hill is built with no grand plan. The hill just emerges as

---

[9] Also see http://www.targetprocess.com/blog/2008/11/agile-software-development-and-complex.html

a result of the termites following a few simple local rules. In a similar way, as organizations go about their normal functions, patterns will begin to emerge—about customers, suppliers, and employees. Spotting these patterns early provides an advantage in terms of meeting customers' changing needs faster than competitors. Therefore, systems should evolve based on how people use them, rather than being imposed from the top down.

- All systems exist within their own environment, and they are also part of that environment. Therefore, as their environment changes, they need to co-evolve—change to ensure a best fit. But because they are part of their environment, when they change, they change their environment, and as it changes, they need to change again; and so it goes on as a constant process (that's why the most successful systems are ironically those that need to change most often). The systems we build today are not designed to be in constant flux—in fact, quite the opposite.

- A complex adaptive system does not have to be perfect in order for it to thrive within its environment. A solution doesn't have to be right, it just has to work. When it stops working, agents tinker their way into another solution. Once it has reached the state of being good enough, a complex adaptive system will trade off increased efficiency every time in favor of greater effectiveness. Yet, we spend an inordinate amount of time trying to get the details right, when it is unlikely to matter very much.

- Complex adaptive systems are not complicated. The emerging patterns may have a rich variety, but like a kaleidoscope, the rules governing the function of the system are quite simple. A classic example is that all the water systems in the world, all the streams, rivers, lakes, oceans, waterfalls, etc. with their infinite beauty, power, and variety are governed by the simple principle that water finds its own level. The flocking behavior of geese (flying in a V-formation) is a popular example of this concept. Geese appear to follow a simple set of rules when flying in formation: don't bump into each other; match up with the speed of the other geese flying nearby; replace the lead goose when it gets tired; always remain with the group. A complex and efficient flying pattern emerges from these few simple rules. Another example: a California school system threw out the detailed rule book and operated with the following three "rules": (1) take care of yourself, (2) take care of others, and (3) take care of this place.

This is in sharp contrast to how we build systems. Our goal is to impose as many rules as possible—so "exceptions" are kept to a minimum.

- Most systems are nested within other systems, and many systems are systems of smaller systems. Consider a food store. The store is itself a system with its staff, customers, suppliers, and neighbors. It also belongs to the food system of that town and the larger food system of that country. It belongs to the retail system locally and nationally, and the economy system locally and nationally. Therefore, it is part of many different systems most of which are themselves part of other systems. As we will see, this ability to nest systems is a critical aspect of building situational applications effectively.

- Life is attracted to order, but it uses chaos to get there. The processes of life have nothing to do with machine efficiencies. They are fuzzy, redundant, and messy. Many solutions are sought in parallel, many individuals are involved in experimentation about the same dilemma. There is no straight line of logic or process that leads to a perfect solution. Instead, there is a great deal of tinkering till someone discovers something that works for now. But the messy processes and fuzzy logic lead to orderly solutions because it is the nature of life to evolve toward more complex and effective systems. Information systems are often too difficult to prototype and experiment with, so this "tinkering" toward a solution simply doesn't happen.

Changing the paradigm

Our Newtonian worldview has led us to focus our efforts on how to get the machine called an organization to work efficiently. Machines are exactly the wrong metaphor for what we need, since machines have no intelligence - they simply follow the instructions given to them, and only work in the specific conditions predicted by their engineers. Changes in their environment wreak havoc because they have no capacity to adapt.

But if we change our thought paradigm, we will start asking a different set of questions and think of different kinds of solutions. If organizations are living systems, then they have many innate capacities, and we need to learn to harness them.

Figure 9: Different starting points for looking at the world.

Ordered World	Complex World
Cause and effect can be precisely determined	Cause and effect are intertwined and cannot be determined in advance
Certain parties have control	All parties have influence

Ordered World	Complex World
There is only one way ahead	There are many possibilities for progress
Large effects require enormous coordinated efforts	Large effects come from small starts and positive feedback
The future can be planned	The future *emerges* from the combined actions of the players

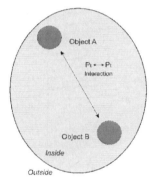

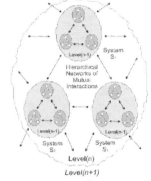

How a "system" is traditionally viewed

(... and how it is "modeled")

- Objects
- Linear
- Homogeneous
- In Equilibrium
- Stable
- Predictable
- Closed to Environment
- Autonomous

How a "system" is viewed as a CAS

(... and what almost all systems are really like)

- Processes
- Nonlinear
- Heterogenous
- Nonequilibrium
- Metastable
- Unpredictable
- Open to Environment
- Interconnected

Figure 10:A CAS is much closer to reality than typical system view.

New Means and New Ways = Transformation

> *"In a revolutionary era of surprise and innovation, you need to learn to think and act like a revolutionary."*

– Joshua Cooper Ramo, *The Age of the Unthinkable*

Until now, if knowledge workers wanted anything more sophisticated than an Excel spreadsheet, they often had no choice but to go to IT:

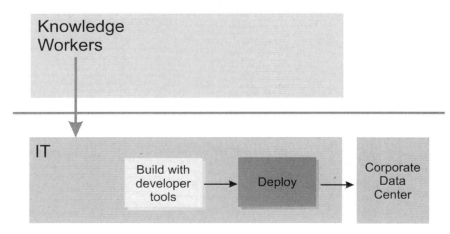

Figure 11: To get an application built, knowledge workers need to go to IT, which has the sole means of production and the means of delivery.

This fits with the tightly controlled, traditional hierarchical organization model followed by most organizations.

The advent of the cloud and the platforms built on top of it are quickly changing this. Instead of building large, complex applications that are made available to knowledge workers to help them do their work, there is now an opportunity to allow the knowledge workers themselves to build their own solutions. From these individual solutions, deployed in the cloud, an enterprise-wide system will emerge.

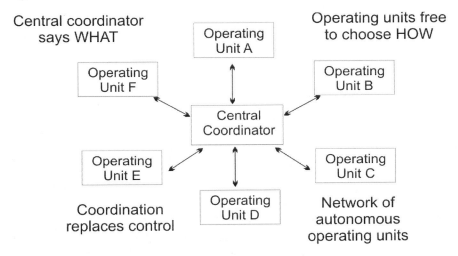

The Responsive Organization is a Network

Figure 12: Each unit is an agent acting to maximize its efficiency.
The total application will emerge from the efforts of each unit.[10]

Once knowledge workers have the tools they need, they can build their own solutions – solutions that are specific to their situation i.e. situational applications. And they have a place where they can deploy the solutions they build – without having to go through a centralized authority, IT. This is a critical, transformational change, and it is facilitated by the advent of the cloud:

---

[10] *Business Agility: Sustainable Prosperity in a Relentlessly Competitive World –* Michael Hugos.

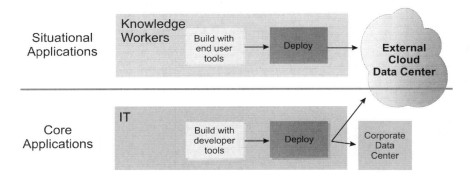

Figure 13: With the cloud, the knowledge worker can build their own solutions and deploy them at will – without impacting or waiting for IT.

Giving knowledge workers the freedom to "do their own thing" within the context of a cloud platform opens up a new world of possibilities for the organization. And it is right in line with the view of the organization as a complex adaptive system – a view that is much better suited to our ceaselessly changing world.

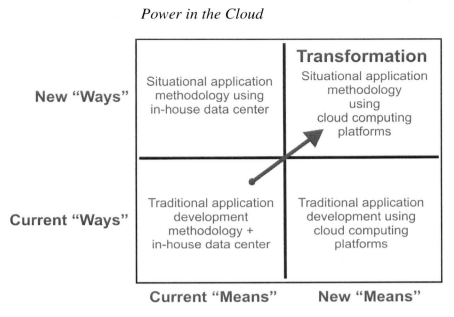

New "Ways" | Situational application methodology using in-house data center | **Transformation** Situational application methodology using cloud computing platforms

Current "Ways" | Traditional application development methodology + in-house data center | Traditional application development using cloud computing platforms

Current "Means" **New "Means"**

Figure 14: Cloud computing + CAS = Transformation

Power in the Cloud

4. An introduction to situational applications

> Sustained competitive advantage will increasingly depend on enabling self-reliant employees to create their own software solutions to meet their business needs.

If we accept Complex Adaptive Systems Theory as our guiding paradigm, and cloud computing as our foundation for moving forward, how do we bring this new approach to building information systems to life?

The situational approach to application building is all about empowering those business users closest to the problems being solved to quickly build full-featured collaborative business applications online and immediately deploy those applications to the appropriate people both inside and outside their organization. This approach allows immediate business challenges to be solved in a cost-effective way by immediately addressing the situation at hand – without the overhead of traditional IT methodology.

In this chapter, we will look at:

- the concept of "situational applications";

- the types of users best suited to build situational applications

- a comprehensive example of a situational application;

- a detailed comparison between the situational and traditional approach to software solutions; and

- the need for a holistic approach to situational applications.

What are situational applications?

> *"Situated software isn't a technological strategy so much as an attitude about closeness of fit between software and its group of users, and a refusal to embrace scale, generality or completeness as unqualified virtues. "*– Clay Shirky

Shriky's aha moment

Clay Shirky is an adjunct professor in New Media at New York University and recently the author of *"Here comes everybody,a book about organizing without organizations."*[11] Back in 2004, he wrote a fascinating article titled "Situated Software."[12] In it, he wrote that he was seeing a change in the "software ecosystem" which he called "situated software," and defined it as "software designed in and for a particular social situation or context."

The key to situated software was that the solution was designed for use by a specific social group, rather than for a generic set of "users." He found that this form-fit solution is significantly cheaper and faster to build and is more likely to be used by its target users.

Shirky provided some insightful examples of situated projects his students had done and these are described later when discussing the situational mindset.

---

[11]   http://www.herecomeseverybody.org/

[12]   http://www.shirky.com/writings/situated_software.html

For Shirky, the term had a definite size dimension (it addressed the needs of a small group of users), as well as a time dimension (it would only be around for a short duration).

IBM moves the ball forward

IBM morphed the term into "situational applications"[13] and defined it as "applications built to address a particular situation, problem, or challenge." IBM added a "who" dimension (non-traditional, casual programmers) and a methodology focusing on time-to-value (short, iterative development life cycles that often are measured in days or weeks) with little up-front emphasis on reliability, scalability, maintainability, and availability.

Morphing further still, it became clear that unlike Shirky's casual student environment, in the enterprise environment, the short time element no longer applied (the application could live a long time), and neither did size (it could be used by many people for a narrow function).

---

[13] http://www.ibm.com/developerworks/webservices/library/ws-soa-situational1/index.html?S_TACT=105AGX04

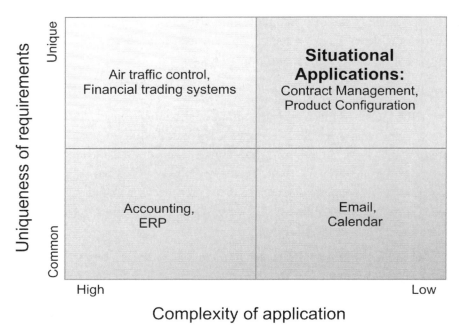

Figure 15: Situational applications have unique, custom requirements, and the complexity of what needs to be done is relatively low.

Cloud computing completes the picture

The advent of cloud computing added yet another dimension – deployment. One of the biggest factors inhibiting the building of sophisticated situational applications has been the need to procure, implement and support a deployment platform. Cloud computing eliminates this problem – applications can be deployed and scaled at will with the click of a button.

A definition of situational applications

In summary, the term "situational application" has now come to represent an alternate approach to building and deploying software solutions. It is about building "good enough" solutions for specific challenges with as little involvement from IT as possible. This is facilitated by cloud-based deployment platforms and high-level application development tools. The result is a dramatic reduction in the time and cost required to go from problem to solution. And when the situation changes, it is easy to change the application.

NOTE: Situationality does not mean a solution is not repeatable. In many instances, the objective will be to automate a business process in the first place so that it can be run multiple times. So it's a situation that repeats itself – sometimes with subtle variations.

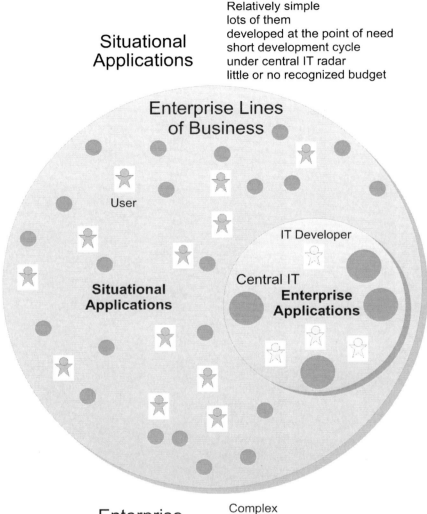

Situational
Applications

Relatively simple
lots of them
developed at the point of need
short development cycle
under central IT radar
little or no recognized budget

Enterprise
Applications

Complex
a few mission critical applications
developed and deployed by central IT
long development deployment cycle
dedicated IT budget

**Figure 16: Situational applications are at the periphery of the organization
(adapted from IBM).**

An example

To understand the potential power of a situational approach to building solutions, let's take the following example. In it, each individual acts on their won to address their particular needs, and a comprehensive, adaptable application emerges. There is no central control, and very little coordination. On the other hand, everyone is working towards the same goal.

Situation

An organization is running a series of seminars. People will register, pay, attend the seminar, and evaluate it. Registrations can be made online or over the phone.

There are a number of different parties involved in making this happen:

- Marketing needs specific types of information to be collected during the registration process to help with creating the seminar agenda.

- The call center needs to know what information to collect when the registration calls come in.

- Management needs to monitor registration levels, and analyze results.

- Accounting needs to track revenue and expenses and, if needed, send invoices to attendees.

- The seminar leader needs to communicate immediately with a registrant as soon as they register.

- The administrator needs to track who actually attends the seminar.

There are primarily two ways to approach this:

1. Use a mixture of Excel spreadsheets, email streams with out-of-date attachments, phone call, lists, etc. There is no central database of information, and therefore no single record of everything related to the seminar. Status checking, searching for information, follow up, etc. - all are done manually, with lots of interruptions disrupting workers.

2. Have IT build an application. An analyst gathers requirements from each person involved, creates a requirements document, gets everyone to sign-off, takes it to IT, which goes through its full development process. Eventually, the system is ready for testing, and then the fun really starts. Of course, there are a whole bunch of changes to be made because users forgot things, or the requirements have changed. Then, using the system causes more changes as it becomes more apparent what was not thought of. Each change results in wasted time and money. Most importantly, IT cannot allocate resources on a timely manner

Clearly, neither of these solutions is very appealing. This is where a situational application platform comes to the rescue.

Solution

Approach

Use a situational application platform to progressively build the application as functionality is needed.

Skill set required

The type of users involved in this example are typical Millennials - they started working with MS Office back in elementary school, and have at least a basic understanding of what a database is.

Building the solution does not require direct IT involvement (beyond possibly the services of a Situational Application Analyst, which is described later).

Tools

This example assumes the organization has selected and supports a situational application platform that meets the criteria to be discussed later.

Action:

Figure 17: The following describes how each person involved takes responsibility for building a small situational application to meet their specific needs. The ultimate application is fairly substantial, and would have taken a significant amount of time to build the traditional way.

Situational Application Scenario	
Who	**What**
Jane, Administrative Assistant	Jane is given the task of arranging seminars for clients. To help her do this, she creates a simple application to track seminar registrations.
	Jane fires up the company's situational application design tool and starts a new application.
	The first thing she does is to specify the information she needs to track. She does this by entering each data field she needs – name, address, etc. The system automatically gives her a complete data entry facility, along with the ability to give permission to other users who may need to access the application. She may run into a little difficulty in figuring out exactly how to structure her data, and calls on a Situational Application Analyst to assist her.

Situational Application Scenario	
Who	**What**
Sam, Call Center telesales rep	Jane is going to outsource the task of getting clients registered to the call center. Sam will be the person responsible in the call center for making the calls and keying in the registrations. Sam finds that the data entry screen Jane set up does not work well when taking registrations over the phone – the fields are in an awkward order, and there are too many screens to navigate through. So Sam opens the application created by Jane, and creates a different version of the data entry screen for himself using a drag-and-drop visual design tool. There is no need to ask Jane or anyone else to do it for him.
Erica, Department Manager	Erica, the department manager, wants to track the registrations as they are made. She goes into the application, selects the data she wants to see, and generates a dashboard gadget in the form of a gauge that shows the number of registrations in real time. With one click, she puts this gadget into her iGoogle portal page and can now watch the number of registrations grow as records are added. She never has to ask Sam or Jane how many registrations have been made at any time.

Situational Application Scenario	
Who	**What**
John, Accounting	John in the accounting department needs to get the billing information into the accounting system. He has permission to access the accounting services available as part of the situational application tool, so he goes ahead and sets up the mapping from the fields he needs, including credit card information and amount.
Frank, Seminar Leader	Frank the seminar leader wants to know every time that someone registers so he can contact them personally. He doesn't need to ask anyone to add this capability to the system for him. He just goes in and adds a simple workflow rule that tells the system to send him an email every time a registration record is added. He also decides he would like Sam to collect an additional piece of information when he takes registrations to help him plan his agenda. He adds the fields he needs, and Sam is automatically informed that this change has taken place in the system. Sam can then adjust his data entry screen as he sees fit.
Jane, Administrative Assistant	Jane needs people to register when they come to the seminar. She adds the additional fields she needs to track this, then creates a simple registration screen. When attendees come to the seminar, they are asked to sign-in using PC's provided. Their sign-ins are immediately registered in the system. No intervention required by anyone else.

Situational Application Scenario	
Who	**What**
Frank, Seminar Leader	At the end of the workshop, Frank wants to send out an evaluation form to be completed by each attendee. He goes into the system and selects an "evaluation" template. He customizes the template to what he needs, and generates a list of attendees from the system. He then emails a link to the evaluation to the attendees. Their responses are recorded and attached to their registration records.

When the evaluations have been completed, he uses built-in reporting and visualization tools to analyze the results. He makes these results available to the rest of the department via a gadget they can add to their portals. |
| Frank, Seminar Leader | A week later, Frank decides to set up an email to go out 3 months after the seminar to each attendee to ask them how they are doing with the things they had learned at the seminar.

To do this, he goes into the system and creates a notification event that associates an email message with the email addresses of the attendees. He specifies when he wants the email to go out. When that time arrives, the system will automatically send out the email. |

The next time the organization wants to run seminars, they have a system ready to go.

Summary

In this example:

- five different people have added their own functionality to the system with little effort;

- they were able to adjust the system themselves to work in ways that met their specific needs;

- they have in effect collaborated without even directly communicating;

- they have been able to build pieces of the system in their own time, at their own pace;

- they are committed to the success of the application – they own it.

From the self-serving actions of multiple individuals working towards a common goal using simple rules, a system emerges.

Caveats

1. Even though this is a relatively simple application, it could grow into quite a substantial application in the future. Therefore, it should be designed as well as possible from the outset. This is certainly not something everyone can do. Hence, as we shall see, there is often a strong need for a "Situational Application Analyst" and a "Seed-Evolve-Reseed" methodology – concepts that will be covered later.

2. There needs to be some protection in place to ensure that other people don't mess up what you have done. This can be a dealt with through a combination of platform constraints and guidelines. Remember, these are small applications, usually for a small group

of people. It's not as though the application has to be protected from invading hordes of potentially damaging users[14].

3. The platform needs to be substantially goal-directed to make this scenario feasible: the user needs to be able to tell the system what they want done without having to figure out how to do it (e.g. "I need to capture data," "I need to send info to accounting," "I need a notification sent to me when people are added to the system"). For more on this, see the section on Goal-Driven Development.

4. While not needed in this particular situation, there is often a requirement for IT to provide external data for situational applications. Plan A (i.e. the best option) is to get direct access to the data through the platform (i.e. the data looks to the user as if it is native to the platform). Plan B is to import the data on a periodic basis. Plan C is to key it in manually (assuming the volume makes it feasible).

There are situational application platforms today that can easily bring this scenario to life.

And think about how much time and effort it would take to build a complete system like this using traditional IT methodology. It would never get done.

The example as a complex adaptive system

The example exhibits many of the characteristics of a CAS:

- The system is self-organizing.

---

14   Also see description of Shirky's students WeBe project.

- It is comprised of semi-autonomous agents.

- It behaves as a unified whole.

- There is no single point of control.

- A pattern (workflow) emerges.

- Communication/connection is built into the system.

- There is potential for unplanned creativity.

- The system evolves and adapts over time based on feedback from the environment.

- Agents act according to certain rules of interaction (they work in the same system development platform which prevents them from stepping on each other's toes).

- The system evolves to maximize "fitness" – in this case, efficiency.

- The system evolves historically – the experience of the agents determines the future trajectory of the system.

- The adaptability of the system can either be increased or decreased by the rules shaping their interaction (e.g. certain users can or cannot get access to certain data).

Target Users

> *"Normal people can and will innovate of their own initiatives if enabling conditions are present."*
> – A. Van de Ven, *The Innovation Journey*

Situational application platforms are aimed primarily at business users, consultants, business analysts, and systems analysts. These users typically have at least some understanding of databases and algorithms, but have neither the time nor inclination to be programmers writing code. However, given the right tools, they can very effectively build software solutions for their organizations in a minimal amount of time and effort.

The building of situational applications can be extended to include less sophisticated business users when they are coupled with a "Situational Application Analyst." For more on this, see the section on methodology.

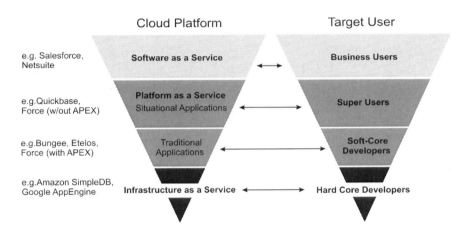

Figure 18: Platform-as-a-Service is split into services aimed at professional developers and services aimed at business users and analysts.

Versus traditional applications

Situational applications are about a never-ending process of being nimble, experimental, dynamic, and continuously iterating. This is in complete contrast to enterprise IT, which is "project focused, do it and forget it."

The following summarizes the primary differences between traditional and situational applications:

Application Characteristics		
	Traditional Application	**Situational Applications**
Development	Developers build applications based on specifications given to them by users.	Users develop applications that are personally meaningful to their work.
Collaboration	Users interact mainly with IT to build solutions	Users collaborate with each other to build shared solutions.
Growth	An application stays in the same form over a period of years.	An application is considered a seed that will evolve continuously.
Participation	Users are recipients of solutions provided by IT (the assumption is that IT has all the relevant knowledge).	Users are not just passive recipients of solutions knowledge, but active contributors, (i.e., they actively co-design and build the application)

Application Characteristics

	Traditional Application	Situational Applications
Contributions	From time to time IT will incorporate new ideas into the application so it doesn't become out of touch with the real world	The application is enriched through the contributions of knowledgeable people, and important and relevant additions are incorporated into the application all the time
Stakeholders	LOB executives, Corporate IT	Individual users/self-organizing small team
Targeted users	Large, generic	A known individual or a small team
Governance	Centralized and formal	Grassroots and community based
Evolution	Top-down controlled, centrally driven, depends on available funding	Organic, based on user feedback and participation
Time-to-value	Many months or years	Days or weeks

Application Characteristics		
	Traditional Application	**Situational Applications**
Development phases	Well defined, following agreed-to schedule (although with frequent schedule overruns)	No defined phases, milestones, or schedules - focus on a good-enough solution to address an immediate need
Functional requirements	Defined by limited number of users; IT needs to "freeze" requirements to move to development; requirement creep often caused by changing business needs	As requirements change, usually changes to accommodate business changes; encourages unintended uses

Application Characteristics		
	Traditional Application	**Situational Applications**
Nonfunctional requirements	Resources allocated to address concerns for performance, availability, and security; focus on these and other nonfunctional requirements (such as scalability and maintainability) often results in robust but costly solutions.	Little or no direct focus on scalability, maintainability, availability, etc., due to nature of platform, significantly reducing cost.
Testing	By IT with some user involvement	By analysts and users
Funding	Often coincides with annual IT planning; requires approved budgets	No formal budget; developed and run under the radar of corporate IT
Stability	Fixed, highly stable	Moving targets and in a state of perpetual beta
Ownership	Controlled environment	Community interest and ownership mentality

Application Characteristics		
	Traditional Application	**Situational Applications**
Adoption	Generalized	Form-fit tools for very particular needs
Communication	Can be a time drain getting everyone involved; larger group means more chance of miscommunication	Smaller group reduces time spent on communication; smaller group means less chance of miscommunication
Problem solving	Solving general problems well requires very careful forethought and planning.	Easier to solve a specific problem e.g. assume only US addresses versus handling global
In depth requirements gathering	Because the cost of developing traditional software is so high, and changes downstream are so rare and costly to implement, there is a huge incentive to develop with other user's needs in mind.	Users develop exactly what they need - this is tremendously freeing for everyone involved

Application Characteristics		
	Traditional Application	**Situational Applications**
Cost	Because the cost is so significant, often need to share cost with others	Software sponsors (users) can spend far less and get exactly what they need.

Figure 19: Traditional and situational applications differ in key areas.

The need for a holistic approach

To get to the point where an organization can successfully build situational applications, it is not enough to simply acquire a tool and hope for the best. Attempting to leverage the power of situational applications by simply tinkering with a tool, adding a system here or there, or putting in another half-baked solution is doomed to failure. **A tool alone will not make a creaky bureaucratic organization into a resilient, intelligent, fast, and flexible organization.**

What is needed is a holistic approach that recognizes the basic tenets of complex adaptive systems theory and results in the empowerment of knowledge workers to build their own solutions within the context of the overall organization.

This includes:

A Mindset

Because applications have always taken a substantial amount of time and effort, there are many potential applications that are ignored because they are seen as too small, of too short duration, too complex or too changeable. There is also the temptation to turn situational applications into generic applications, and to make situational applications as robust and user-friendly as traditional applications. A new mindset, based on CAS, is needed to ensure that we do not go down familiar paths so we can get the most out of situational applications.

A Methodology

The traditional IT methodology is ill-suited to building situational applications. The goal of situational applications is to eliminate as much IT overhead as possible. This needs to be balanced by ensuring that end users get the support they need to build their own solutions.

A Platform

To facilitate the building of situational applications, the appropriate platform needs to be adopted. This platform needs to have the appropriate enabling capabilities, as well as specific functionality that can make the building and deployment of solutions as easy as possible.

We'll look at each of these in turn. But first, let's take a look at what can be built with a situational application approach.

5. From the Trenches:
An Enabling Technology

Kevin Smith of *Nextwave Performance:*

Like the web itself, situational application platforms are an "enabling technology" – a technology that through its very existence allows the creation of applications that otherwise would never have existed. They allow non-coder users to take their ideas and turn them into reality with very little development overhead.

For example, my consulting practice has a methodology for process improvement that has been honed over 15 years or so. We've always had the dream of developing software to help execute this methodology, but traditional development has been cost prohibitive. We determined that we'd need several developers - each with an ownership stake in our company - and 6 to 9 months of development time to get the first beta out the door. This, combined with the other start-up and operational costs would necessitate a price per user that significantly higher than what we wanted to charge. Then we found a situational application platform. I used it to build a suite of integrated applications that did exactly what we wanted *WITHOUT* developers, *WITHOUT* servers, *WITHOUT* giving away the company, and – it took less than 90 days.

Had we not had this platform, we never would have even attempted to develop the application. It allows non-coders to turn ideas that otherwise wouldn't have seen the light of day into reality. To suggest that traditional development tools and techniques will suffice misses the point and does the platform as a whole a great injustice.

Power in the Cloud

6. How to leverage situational applications

"Cloud Computing makes it possible to create new 'business operations platforms' that will allow companies to change their business models and collaborate in powerful new ways with their customers, suppliers and trading partners – stuff that simply could not be done before." – Peter Fingar, *Dot.Cloud: The 21st Century Business Platform*

So if you could build and deploy solutions on demand, what would you do? Every company has hundreds of opportunities for improvement. But sometimes they are hard to see and a little more digging and analysis is required – especially since everyone is heads-down and focused on getting their everyday job done.

In this chapter, we will explore different ways to find situational applications in your company. It is divided as follows:

- Different types of applications that lend themselves to a situational approach.

- How situational applications can help.

- A simple model to help anyone analyze any "situation" in order to improve it.

Situational application patterns

"In an endless pursuit of innovation, companies of thousands of employees, and sole proprietors alike, strive to distinguish themselves, and avoid commoditization so they can demand a premium for their goods and services." – Peter Fingar, *Extreme Competition*

The following is a breakdown of the typical types of situational applications that can be built. Actual examples are provided in the Case Studies section. The objective of this section is to spark ideas to help find potential situational applications in your organization.

Knowledge packaging

The goal is to embed knowledge into an application in order to eliminate the need to involve expensive resources when it is unnecessary. For example, a cable company needs to qualify leads based on how close a prospect is to an access point. Creating an application that instantly provides "distance scores" for each new lead and the associated potential construction costs provides immediate information directly to salespeople without involving anyone from the engineering department.

This type of savings is available in almost every organization. Take the example of a market research company where the salespeople need to get input from many different departments to put together a single quote for a client. Every time the specifications change, the salesperson has to go back to each department. The amount of time wasted and the delays incurred can be enormous.

One of the major advantages of situational platforms is that each department can take responsibility for automating and maintaining their part of the bidding process. Because each department does this on the same platform, it is much easier to then bring together each separate solution into a cohesive whole.

Also, once the knowledge required to estimate a job has been packaged, it may be possible to give (particularly existing) clients the ability to estimate jobs on their own, and initiate an order process immediately – without any human involvement.

Another example is manufacturing where, for example, the salesperson has to gather detailed requirements from the user in order to configure a product they require. It is extremely difficult for salespeople to know that when part A is selected, then part B can go with it, but not part C. Inevitably, there is significant back-and-forth with the engineering department for the salesperson to clarify what is needed.

Data Entry

Building situational applications that are specific to the type of data being entered, how it is being entered, and by whom it is being entered can ensure that it does not have to be re-checked later in the process, or that it will cause unforeseen exceptions later on, or that it will have to be re-keyed into other systems.

Situational applications for data entry can have a significant impact and can usually be done with minimal effort. Here are a few variations:

One source, multiple destinations

There is a single source of data for an application (e.g. a client), but the user needs to enter data into multiple systems. The solution is to build a front-end application that captures all the information in a single place and feeds the data into all the systems that need it, thereby reducing errors and time.

Improved navigation

Data entry screens are often:

- confusing;

- contain fields that aren't needed by the person doing the data entry;

- contain fields that are in the wrong sequence for easy entry;

- force the user to move back and forth unnecessarily among multiple screens.

A typical symptom of this type of problem is seen where information is written down on a piece of paper and keyed in later –wasting time and prone to error. A situational application can clean up screens to make it much faster and easier for the user to enter data.

Data vetting

Situational applications can be built to thoroughly vet data to ensure correctness from the start. This can significantly eliminate potential problems down the line.

Consolidation

Billions of dollars are lost every year because information systems do not work together. A vast amount of unnecessary time is spent in every office in every corner of the world just trying to act as the glue between systems.

This is particularly true when a single task that needs to be done requires information from more than one system. This means that the user has to take the time to compose the information they need to complete the task. Not only does it waste time, it is prone to error and can impair decision making.

Situational applications are well suited to these scenarios because no one knows the situation facing business users better than the users themselves. If they are able to build applications by pulling information from enterprise applications, departmental applications and even desktop applications, they could significantly increase their productivity.

Adoption

When a user is inhibited from taking a course of action that is desired by the company (because it is e.g. too difficult for them to do or it requires extra work), chances are it is not going to get done.

A simple example is what happens when you go to a movie theatre. The movie theatre wants to sell you a "combo," because that way they make a higher profit. But if it means that the person behind the counter needs to do extra work to fulfill a combo order, chances are they won't make offering it a high priority, and even if they do, it will slow down the fulfillment process.

Creating situational applications to make it easier to e.g. bundle services and package products can go a long way to helping ensure that the practices you want to encourage are adopted.

Self-service

Self service applications are a simple way to reduce costs and improve service. Perhaps the best example is FedEx allowing customers to track packages from their Web sites, with no human intervention required. Leveraging and linking systems to automate processes for answering inquiries from customers dramatically reduced the cost of serving them while increasing their satisfaction and loyalty.

There are different self-service areas that situational applications can address:

Status checking. Allow the client to check the status of their orders, the progress of their project, the status of insurance claims.

Knowledge access. Allow users to enter parameters and get answers they need. E.g. find nearby clinics by specialty and distance.

Data entry and maintenance. Allow customers and partners to take responsibility for entering their own orders, support requests, etc....

Rollup and consolidation

There are many instances where data needs to be collected from multiple sources and then consolidated into a single system. Often, each source has slightly different ways of doing things, but the information required by the central system is the same.

Situational applications can be developed to take into account the unique needs of each source, and still automatically collect the common data that is required from all. An obvious example is budgeting – each department can budget their own way, but still feed the common numbers needed from all department.

Once automated, additional functionality can easily be added that significantly improves efficiency. For example, automated reminders can be implemented to ensure that the information needed is made available in a timely fashion. Another possible advantage is the ability of the central function to get real-time visibility on what is happening at each source location.

Mashups

> *"Mashups aren't invented during the IT department's annual offsite meetings. Instead, they spring from the minds of entrepreneurial virtuosos who are continually sifting through the services they discover on the Internet and imagining the emergent possibilities." – Mashup Corporations: The End of Business as Usual,* Andy Mulholland, Chris S. Thomas, Paul Kurchina

Mashups combine similar types of media and information from multiple sources into a single representation. A typical example is combining customer address data with Google Maps to show locations and print directions.

While there are tools that are designed specifically to do mashups, most situational application platforms are able to build mashups.

Situational applications that mash together disparate data in unique ways can be extremely powerful. Kelly Shaw from Serena provides a great example of a data mashup application in her blog.[15]

---

[15] http://businessmashup.blogspot.com/2007/10/how-close-are-we-to-overcoming-10.html

"Assume I run a fleet of ice cream trucks and I want to make the best use of the trucks. I could use a presentation or data mashup to help by pulling local event information from online community calendars, school activity calendars, business announcements and even law enforcement announcements. I could map these events on a Google Map along with information about the likely size and times of the events. Using this information I could develop a schedule to optimize the routes of my trucks.

... [I could also] take the information from the mashup and use it automatically to schedule trucks, drivers and inventory to make sure the right trucks were at the right locations with the right inventory at the right time. ... [The application] would know when trucks are due for maintenance and schedule the maintenance around heavy usage days based on the mashed-up information."

In this example, external data is mixed with enterprise data to produce actionable information that would not otherwise be feasible.

Giving users the access to different types of data that they can then mash into applications that are meaningful specifically to them open up extremely powerful opportunities for significantly increasing the efficiency of the organization.

Unbundling

Situational applications are particularly valuable where companies segment work into discrete tasks for independent contractors and then re-aggregate the results of that work.

Examples include: health care delivery, where elements of the process (e.g. reading x-rays) are handed off to external contractors who must have access to certain data, and return other data upon completion of their discrete task; buying fractional time on a jet, in a high-end sports car, or even for designer handbags; and on the supply side, with asset-intensive businesses like factories, warehouses, truck fleets, office buildings, data centers, networks, etc., where utilization rates can be raised.

Companies can more easily harvest the talents of others working outside corporate boundaries if they can rapidly create highly custom applications that cater to the specific needs of each relationship. This makes it more feasible to involve customers, suppliers, small specialist businesses, and independent contractors in the creation of products and services.

These applications allow companies to give substantial leeway to outsiders while still maintaining overall visibility and control over what is being done. This can substantially reduce costs and help get new products to market faster by eliminating the bottlenecks that come with inefficient communication mechanisms and processes.

Shifting more work to freelancers and outsiders and unbundling assets will also lead to new pricing models that will need to be tracked and adjusted frequently. It will not be possible to involve IT in every change that needs to be made to support this growing trend.

Value-added services

Surrounding commodity items with a tailored blanket of value-added services can transform your business. By turning your products into tailored solutions that solve important problems for your customers, you can sell your products for a few percentage points more than your competitors.

Michael Hugos, in his book *Business Agility: Sustainable Prosperity in a Relentlessly Competitive World,*[16] provides the perfect real-life example of how this can work in his example of "The Value-Added Paper Cup."

When he was the chief information officer of a national distributor of food-service disposables and janitorial supplies (like paper cups), his challenge was to make the products more valuable and earn a higher profit. He and his team devised a menu of about 50 different value-added services that salespeople could then mix and match to meet specific customer needs.

The services included:

- Making it very easy and convenient for customers to find and order cups by providing an online product catalog that let them search on many different product parameters (size, strength, color, materials used, etc.).

- Automatically reminding them to order other items that normally go along with cups, such as lids and sleeves.

- Placing and tracking their orders online so they could know when their supplies would be delivered.

- Sending invoices in whatever format customers wanted so they could automatically import them into their accounts payable systems.

---

[16] *Business Agility: Sustainable Prosperity in a Relentlessly Competitive World, by Michael Hugos.* Wiley, 2009.

- Inserting customers' general ledger codes into every line item on invoices so those costs could be automatically disbursed to their general ledger systems.

- Providing customers with easy-to-use Web-based reporting that let them see how many cups (and other products too) they ordered at each of their ordering locations over any period of time, from one day to two years.

- Providing customers with the ability to monitor their spending and get detailed data for planning and budgeting, along with real-time insight into usage patterns and purchasing trends.

- Negotiate a set of service-level agreements (SLAs) with customers and then using a simple business process management (BPM) system and some Web-based dashboards to track the company's actual performance against customer SLA's. The business process management system compared customer purchase orders with advance ship notices and invoices to automatically calculate the performance statistics displayed on the dashboards (things like order fill rates, on-time delivery rate, and perfect order rates).

Every company has its equivalent of the paper cup.

Touchpoint streamlining

An organization's touchpoints refer to its interactions with customers, suppliers and employees. They involve the interface between the organizational structure and a person or persons. Each touch-point represents a significant area of potential process or quality improvement, and competitive advantage. Most importantly, touchpoints represent areas where human interaction is often at its most intense.

Touchpoints can be regarded as the periphery of an enterprise's central nervous system. As in human anatomy, it is the extremities that define the efficiency of our interaction with the world around us. Dexterity, mobility, and adaptability depend primarily on the nimbleness of our peripheral nervous system; fingers, toes, hands, feet, arms, and legs define how well we can react to events around us. In this same way an enterprise may have outstanding strategies, plans, and tactics, but they must be enabled, through actions taken to satisfy customers, educate and leverage workers, and negotiate trade with suppliers.

To make these touchpoints more effective, it is critical to streamline the tiresome and repetitive tasks that otherwise consume employees' time and energy. Even a slight application of the right technology in these areas can have an extraordinary impact on a company's processes.

If it is easy enough to do, employees are far more likely to constantly refine the way interactions are completed at the touchpoints of the organization, making them faster and include more value for the other party. Enriching and streamlining individual transactions at the lowest level is something that will be difficult for competitors to replicate.

Innovation facilitation

Finding new and creative ways to solve business problems is key to remaining competitive. Until now, there have often been too many barriers to putting in place the software solutions you need to support the innovation. IT doesn't have the bandwidth and you don't have the knowledge or resources to build the solutions you need. Now with situational applications, you can break outside the box and do it yourself. Who knows better than you what your business problems are? Why shouldn't you create the solution?

Email tag elimination

There are many situations in every organization where the game of email tag consumes time and delays action. For example, a salesperson wants to generate a quote for a customer and include it in a proposal. Depending on the discount given, there are various levels of management approval needed. So the salesperson sends an e-mail to their boss asking to approve a 10% discount. The manager sends an email back to the salesperson asking for the rationale behind the discount. The salesperson responds. The manager e-mails a sales executive to get their approval. A few days later the salesperson checks up on the status of the approval (if they remember to do so), and another flurry of e-mails occurs. Finally, the discount is approved. The salesperson can now create the proposal and send to the customer. At the end of the quarter, sales ops wants to track discounts over 5%. They e-mail all sales managers asking for a report of discounts over 5%.

Clearly, using this process made up of email, spreadsheets, and manual reviews is not very efficient.

In the situational application solution, an employee fills out a simple web form. The system automatically connects to people or systems to ensure the business information is reviewed, approved or denied, routed, and placed into the appropriate business system.

In this example, we can enable the automation, coordination, and collaboration of a simple proposal request, and delivered a much simpler process that, in turn, increased the efficiency and productivity within the organization.

Monitoring

Situational applications are very useful to people who need to "keep an eye on" volatile data, like currency exchange rates, or things like machine availability, today's sales, or inventory levels. Situational applications that are delivered as widgets[17] allow you to set up small monitoring tools that watch data values while you go on with other work on the rest of your screen. Widgets create a consistent framework for monitoring, and allow for applications like combining everything you're monitoring into one window, setting alert thresholds when something changes too much, and easily sharing such tools with others even in different companies.

Repetitive tasks

Situational applications deployed as widgets can be particularly effective for repetitive tasks that are done "off to the side," like creating a new user account, resetting a password, changing an address, approving a purchase requisition, etc. With widgets, users can perform

---

[17] Widgets are micro applications that can easily be placed on a web page. They are usually designed to solve a very specific problem for a specific type of user. They are quick and easy to build, customize, deploy and share. Widgets are important because they fundamentally change the way that content (and functionality) is disseminated over the Web - instead of going from site to site, users can do what they need from the comfort of their own personal Web page. For more on widgets, see the Appendix.

these common actions quickly, in a compact and simple interface, without interrupting the other work open on their computer.

Raving fans

Situational applications can be a useful mechanism for helping to create "raving fans[18]." People like to be remembered, and valued. But it is very difficult in the day-to-day rush of things to be done to remember to take the time to send out a thank-you note, or a letter asking how things are working out with the product you purchased, or the service you received.

A situational application can be used to do all these things and more. For example, an organization of pediatric occupational therapists built a situational application that automatically sent an email to its patients on their birthdays. The email contained a video of their therapists singing happy birthday. It was simple to build – the system already knew the patients birth date and who their therapist was. Once the video was made (a 1 minute exercise), it was set to go. This is an example of how you create raving fans – and grow your business.

Other ways include:

- **Making it easier (and more pleasant) for customers to do business with you**. One way is to provide them with systems that are tailored more specifically to their exact needs.

- **Knowing what your customers want by giving them an easy way to tell you**. A simple application to collect,

---

[18] *Raving Fans: A Revolutionary Approach To Customer Service*, by Ken Blanchard & Sheldon Bowles

categorize and rank customer ideas could go a long way to help make this happen.

- **Knowing better who your customers are.** Collect and analyze information about them so you can better cater to their needs. To do this, build applications that automatically send out questions and follow-ups, and produce meaningful reports.

- **Making your clients feel that you really care**. For example, sending out the birthday video in the example above.

Continuity

Continuity is all about making sure nothing falls through the cracks. This can be done by sending instant notifications of events within a workflow to one or many users, and allowing users to monitor the progress of instances through the stages of workflow and see what everyone's roles and responsibilities are. This allows for a faster response to staff, customers or partners.

Situational Application Modeling

Since situational applications are all about addressing each situation effectively, it makes sense to break down a "situation" and evaluate all its elements. This is the ultimate way to build an application from the bottom up. A major advantage of a situational application platform is that it facilitates this type of approach.

The following is a simple model to help anyone analyze a "situation" in order to improve it.

For example:

1. Select an employee in e.g. customer service.

2. Identify a specific set of situations that they confront as part of their job.

3. Analyze each situation by using the questions suggested by the model.

4. Based on the analysis, identify what types of situational applications could be built to make this person more productive.

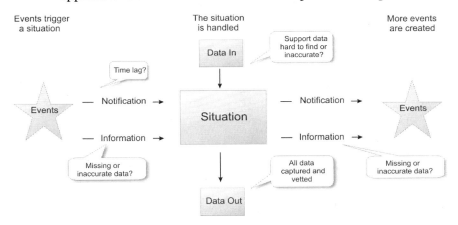

Figure 20: This is a simple situational application model that can be used to analyze any "situation."

There are many questions that can be asked that will elicit how this situation can be improved. For example:

1. What event(s) triggers the situation? e.g. a client calls to ask for the status of their rebate check.

2. Do you have *all* the information you need about the situation before you start handling it?

3. Do you have easy access to supporting information that will help you deal with the situation?

4. If you have to search for data to handle the situation, can you do this efficiently?

5. Is everyone who needs to know made aware of how you handled the situation?

6. If you create a new event, are the right people/systems automatically notified that they need to take action now or in the future?

7. Are you capturing the right information about the situation so that it can be used as needed later?

8. Are there actions that could be taken to take advantage of the situation? E.g. if the situation is handling a customer complaint, automatically send the customer a follow-up email in a week.

9. Are the results of how the situation is handled always positive? If not, why not? What can be done to improve the chances of success?

Notes:

Situational Application Modeling (SAM) mixed with a situational application platform is the ultimate bottom-up approach to building applications. It is not meant to be a substitute for business process management (BPM) which takes a top-down view. SAM is not designed to re-engineer a whole process. It can lead to a re-engineering of a process, but it comes about as a result of improving each person's efficiency *within* the existing process.

Where situational applications can help

"Now picture a huge, heavy flywheel. It's a massive, metal disk mounted horizontally on an axle. It's about 100 feet in diameter, 10 feet thick, and it weighs about 25 tons. That flywheel is your company. Your job is to get that flywheel to move as fast as possible, because momentum – mass times velocity – is what will generate superior economic results over time.

"Right now, the flywheel is at a standstill. To get it moving, you make a tremendous effort. You push with all of your might, and finally, you get the flywheel to inch forward. After two or three days of sustained effort, you get the flywheel to complete one entire turn. You keep pushing, and the flywheel begins to move a bit faster. It takes a lot of work, but at last the flywheel makes a second rotation. You keep pushing steadily. It makes three turns, four turns, five, six. With each turn, it moves faster, and then -- at some point, you can't say exactly when -- you break through. The momentum of the heavy wheel kicks in your favor. It spins faster and faster, with its own weight propelling it. You aren't pushing any harder, but the flywheel is accelerating, its momentum building, its speed increasing." – Jim Collins, Author, *Good to Great*

Situational applications typically address small amounts of productivity or automation that result in a large future value impact on your business. Many small gains over time create compounding efficiency.

It is often hard to see or remember all the different things that can be improved. Here are some of the typical areas that situational applications can help:

Improve decision making

- Increase the speed by which knowledge workers receive information;

- deliver the right information to the right person at the right time;

- provide shared, common access to the latest information at all times;

- automatically consolidate information from multiple sources;

- increase the speed with which the knowledge worker receives fresh information;

- isolate the specific information each knowledge worker needs so they don't have to look for it and extract it themselves;

- ensure employees are aware of pertinent information at all times.

Reduce errors

- Reduce re-keying of information by providing single data entry facilities for multiple systems;

- provide a central shared database to ensure everyone is working off the same data at all times;

- eliminate paperwork by providing online forms;

- allow the sources of information to enter information themselves (e.g. customers entering their own orders);

- prevent things from falling through the cracks through automated notification of missed deadlines;

- deal with problems earlier by automating red-flag reporting through monitoring (e.g. automatic reporting prompts the appropriate user to take action, like when a project is overdue or over-spent).

Reduce cycle time

- Improve visibility of commitments so decisions aren't delayed due to missed commitments or poor coordination;

- reduce miscommunication by keeping the right data, making it always available, and by making changes immediately visible;

- reduce lag time by automatically notifying the next person in a workflow to start a process (e.g. once a warehouse employee marks all items in an order as received, an e- mail goes to the delivery scheduling department, allowing them to start processing the order immediately without human intervention);

- bring together all the information required from inside and outside the enterprise, then remixing it allows users to solve situational problems quickly;

- save time by reducing unnecessary communication like asking others for status updates;

- increase the use of systems by personalizing them to the exact needs of the users;

- reduce extra work to do what is best e.g. if it best to sell bundles or packages of products. But if it is too difficult for the user to do it, they won't do it. E.g. combo in a movie theatre. Need 1 button for the combo.

Provide better information faster

- Ensure accuracy of that information by having clients take responsibility for entering and maintaining it;

- improve timeliness of client information – they can update it themselves when their information changes;

- by providing quick access to data through a single, easily accessible repository and personalized views and reports, search time can be reduced significantly.

Reduce costs

- Make data collection more convenient by providing access through widgets and mobile devices;

- eliminate incomplete paper forms by providing consistent data entry screens, with required and validated fields;

- improve collaboration to facilitate the transfer, sharing and simultaneous processing of information;

- make clients responsible for entering and maintaining their own information;

- build applications that allow partners, clients and employees to serve themselves.

Improve attention allocation

- Reduce the need to do constant follow-up by using automated notifications;

- reduce the need to search for information – make the information come directly to the user when they need it;

- reduce the amount of clutter the user needs to push through to get the exact information they need.

- track assignments and issue automatic alerts to ensure all team members know exactly what they're responsible for.

Increase customer satisfaction

- Improve customer loyalty by making the client feel that you care specifically about *their* unique needs (e.g. create highly customized solutions for each client);

- respond faster to customer queries by making information easy to find;

- provide customers with the ability to serve themselves;

- automatically keep the customer informed through automated notifications;

- decrease miscommunication by increasing visibility into processes that impact the customer;

- identify problem trends early by automating data monitoring of customer-related activities.

Increase competitiveness

- Gain insight by unlocking and re-mixing information in new ways;

- make it easier and less costly to try new ideas;

- free up more time for innovation by automating common tasks;

- make it easier to implement new services – and withdraw them easier – lower sunk cost;

- make it faster, cheaper, easier to build prototypes;

- facilitate disaggregation of services – make it easier to split up work that can then be outsourced and reintegrated;

- promote innovation by empowering users to author their own solutions;

- increase agility by dynamically assemble new applications and bring them to market quickly in order to respond to changing conditions;

- reduce missed commitments by improving the visibility of commitments and automating the notification of missed deadlines.

Increase employee satisfaction

- Reduce stress through automation;

- provide software that is better suited to each users unique needs;

- provide users with the ability to create their own solutions;

- provide easier access to enterprise and Web data for use in their job;

- improve the coordination of work amongst employees;

- provide critical insight into the status of projects, sales goals and other objectives, helping to identify potential issues early on;

- identify problem trends earlier by e.g. automatically triggering alerts when jobs fall off schedule so corrective action can be taken to get back on track quickly.

Improve IT-Business alignment

- Rapid prototyping provides improved communication and requirements sharing, leading to more customer-focused applications;

- support self-service capabilities, especially for Millennials;

- use situational application tools to deliver certain types of applications faster and cheaper and using lower, less expensive skills.

Power in the Cloud

7. The situational application mindset

"I have found that in nearly all situations I can view what is happening in Complex Adaptive Systems terms and that this opens up a variety of new options which give me more choice and more freedom." – Peter Fryer, *Trojan Mice*

To leverage situational applications effectively, it is critical to recognize and understand how a mindset based on complex adaptive systems theory differs from a traditional mindset.

But first we will delve into the 2 critical elements of a situational (and CAS) mindset: "good enough" and "closeness of fit."

What is "good enough?"

Clay Shirky describes a simple project undertaken by his students that very clearly illustrates the concept of "good enough" software. The WeBe application is an excellent example of why a situational application is so much less expensive and time-consuming to build.

WeBe is a simple tool for enabling college students to coordinate and purchase things as a group.

Because money was involved, the traditional approach would require some way of dealing with the threat of non-payment, using things like pre-pay or escrow accounts, or formal reputation systems. Instead, the decision was made that since all the users were part of the community that application was built for, they would simply make it easy to track the deadbeats, with the threat of public broadcast of their names.

The solution was "good enough" – the application didn't have to take into account and deal with all the exceptions that might occur. This was a much less expensive way to deal with this issue that did not require any development at all – and may never have to be invoked given the small scale involved. But the application had real value for the group it was intended to service, and would probably not have been built at all if this type of condition needed to be catered for by the application.

The situational mindset resists the temptation to ask questions like: "Why not make it as broadly accessible as possible?" For traditional applications, the answer is usually "No reason," since more users are always, as Shirky says, "A Good Thing." But for situational applications, this type of thinking is deadly and can stop worthwhile situational applications projects in their tracks. As in this case, the size and cohesion of the user community, for example, can eliminate a lot of functionality that would need to be introduced if generalized.

What is "closeness of fit?"

"Situated software isn't a technological strategy so much as an attitude about closeness of fit between software and its group of users, and a refusal to embrace scale, generality or completeness as unqualified virtues."

The problem with traditional software is that it is often built for a generic user. Allowing the user to customize the interface of a Web site might make it more useful, but it doesn't make it any more personal than the ATM putting your name on the screen while it spits out your money.

Situational applications, by contrast, don't need to be personalized – they are personal from inception. The application's lack of generality or completeness, in other words, communicates something – "We built this for you."

One of Shirky's students mentioned building a web application for his mother, a schoolteacher, to keep track of her class. Making an application specifically for your mom is very different than writing an application that would satisfy the general and complete needs of schoolteachers everywhere.

The situational mindset resists the temptation to elevate a local solution to serve the whole organization or every client, etc.

Versus the traditional mindset

> Change is the organizing force, not a problematic intrusion.

The following contrasts a situational mindset with the traditional mindset. Many of these points are consistent with CAS theory:

Figure 21: Situational applications require a different way of thinking.

Mindset		
	Traditional applications	**Situational applications**
Embrace incrementalism	Because the overhead of starting up an IT project is so great, it only makes sense to tackle large projects with a significant payback.	A situational application is never going to have the impact of a single application, like ERP. But the incremental impact of a multitude of small situational applications can result in geometric growth in productivity.
Embrace messiness	Messiness is the scourge of IT.	Highly adaptable systems may look sloppy. There is no point in wasting resources and energy trying to make something look beautiful if it's not going to be around for very long or is going to change all the time.

Mindset		
	Traditional applications	**Situational applications**
Use simplifying assumptions	Because of the time and cost involved, there is a need to try anticipate the needs of "any" user and anticipate every contingency.	Situational applications are aimed at a very specific target audience, assumptions that simplify the application can be made e.g. building applications without a lot of security, authentication, etc. because it will be used by a small user community who know and trust each other.
Get personal, don't personalize	A significant amount of time and effort is put into both making a system generic as well as providing a way to "personalize" it. This makes the application much more complex than if it were written for a specific use.	Situational applications don't need to be personalized – they are personal from inception. The applications lack of generality or completeness, communicates that "this was built this for you."

Mindset		
	Traditional applications	**Situational applications**
Re-think ROI	Because of the significant cost involved, calculating ROI is essential.	The cost of justifying the return on investment for developing small services will, in many cases, be more costly than developing the service in the first place. For example, no one would do an ROI for a spreadsheet.
Embrace change	Change is the enemy of traditional applications. Requirements are frozen in time, and are only changed with great reluctance, because change creates a cascading affect across the various roles involved in the process (QA, documentation, etc.).	Solutions are recognized from the start to be temporary and are treated as such. The system can be made to respond to any situation. There are few negatives to implementing change

Mindset		
	Traditional applications	**Situational applications**
Underprescribe	The tendency in traditional development is to overprescribe – to think of all the possible exceptions and variations that might occur and cater for them when the system is written. This is important for applications where efficiency is key.	Most business processes involving knowledge workers are fluid and adaptable, so they cannot be too restrictive. This would also likely encourage rigidity due to a lack of desire to change the things needed to deal with exceptions. So the goal is to keep Situational applications "elegantly minimal"—to create "elbow room" for local interpretations and innovations.
Be specific	To help justify the cost and to try to reduce the chance of changes later, every conceivable scenario needs to be considered.	Build for a very specific set of users and features.

Mindset		
	Traditional applications	**Situational applications**
Seek success	Traditional applications by their nature are focused on seeking to avoid failure and are concerned about keeping things status quo.	By being able to easily adapt, situational applications are focused on seeking success and finding new, better ways to perform tasks.
Status quo	Because of the cost to change, there is a strong prejudice towards keeping the status quo.	Because it is easy to change, there is an impetus to find new ways to perform better.
Self-organize (start projects up at will)	Because of the number of people involved, the cost and planning that needs to take place to deliver a traditional application, self-organization is not an option.	One of the key determinants of situational applications is the amount of leeway users have to "do their own thing."

Mindset		
	Traditional applications	**Situational applications**
Start simple	Because of the built-in overhead associated with starting up a traditional application development project, it is difficult to justify taking on only a sub-set of an application.	Because applications can be built and abandoned quickly, they can be delivered informally, starting with a very crude version 1, then iterated rapidly.
Re-think longevity	We assume applications should work for long periods in part because it costs so much to create them.	Once it's cheap and easy to throw together an application, longevity doesn't matter. Businesses routinely ask teams of well-paid people to put hundreds of hours of work creating a single PowerPoint deck that will be looked at in a single meeting. The idea that software should be built for many users, or last for many years, are cultural assumptions not required by the software itself.

Power in the Cloud

8. The Situational Application Methodology

> *"Ideas for new solutions will spring from half-baked applications created by lay users who may start down the path toward a solution, but may lack the expertise to finish it." – Mashup Corporations: The End of Business as Usual,* Andy Mulholland, Chris. S. Thomas, Paul Kurchina

IT organizations are geared toward the development, support and deployment of wide-scale applications. It therefore only makes sense to tackle large projects with a significant payback. Conversely, the overhead of an IT project eliminates the feasibility of many smaller projects.

The goal of situational applications is to eliminate as much IT overhead as possible. This needs to be balanced by ensuring that end users get the support they need to build their own solutions.

Unless a much lighter methodology is used, a great many opportunities are going untapped due to returns that won't exceed initial investment in any reasonable timeframe.

In this chapter, we'll look at:

- why we need a very different methodology to build situational applications;

- how situational methodology differs from traditional methodology;

- what a situational methodology looks like.

Railroads versus Taxicabs

"It is possible to set up organizations so that when I am pursuing my own self-interest, I automatically benefit everyone else, whether I mean to or not."
– Abraham Maslow

Historically, information has been delivered to desktops in much the same fashion as railroads were built in the early 1900s. Building a railroad system required multiple stages of planning, agreed-upon destinations, predetermined stops at train stations, limited switching choices, the moving of businesses closer to the stations, and rigid schedules to maximize rail efficiency rather than user demand. The very nature of the railroad system leaves little room for flexibility and adaptability. This characteristic is critically important for railroads - and certain types of business applications such as accounting and manufacturing.

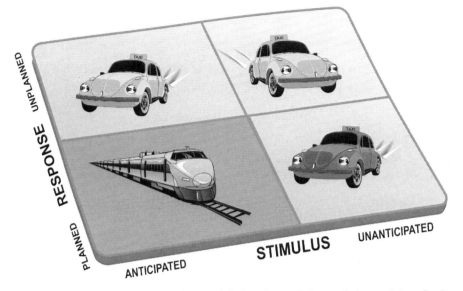

Figure 22: Railway systems require careful planning and the result is pre-determined. Running taxi cabs requires little planning and the results are completely indeterminate.

But this approach, with its fixed plans, fixed rails, stations, and pre-determined schedules, doesn't work when events cannot be easily anticipated and responses need to be made up on-the-fly. The need for a dynamic business environment is more closely reflected in the process that taxi cab companies use to respond to demand. In a typical U.S. city, cabs cruise the streets with only flexible strategies, allowing response to demand to unfold as required. Decisions are made as closely as possible to the time when action must be taken. The driver makes decisions on the spot - consistent with passengers needs.

In the railroad "methodology," the organization plans in advance and passengers must adjust their plans accordingly. In the taxicab approach, the organization must adjust in real time to the passenger whose plans are unknown most of the time. This requires organizations to embrace uncertainty, dynamic demand, and some degree of chaos, and to learn to thrive on it.

The rest is left to the flexibility, adaptability, and creativity of the individual agents as the context continually changes.

This, of course, is a frightening thought for many. But the key questions are: Are these traditional metaphors working for us today? Are we able today to lay out detailed plans and then "just do it" with a guaranteed outcome? If not, do we really think that building systems will get any better?

IT department managers—who have justifiable concerns with reliability and availability of corporate systems, data privacy, and security and who are faced with decreasing budgets—often tend to be conservative in their adoption of new technologies and agile development methods. As a result, corporate IT is often seen as unable to support the business and can be perceived as a hindrance to rather than an enabler of innovation.6 During the last 30 years, while languages, platforms, and tools have changed significantly, IT solution-development processes have changed very little.

But to achieve the levels of functionality, flexibility, and time-to-market required by knowledge workers, a radical shift is required in the way in which software is developed. Technology alone will not make any serious impact on the speed and effectiveness with which we are able to build information systems. We need a more appropriate methodology. Situational applications need to be created without the overhead and formality of traditional information technology methods.

When users are no longer constrained by the shackles of inflexible information systems and are instead empowered by them to act as independent agents pursuing their own solutions with minimal central control, new, highly competitive, and formidable business enterprises can emerge.

The problems with traditional methodology

Process versus Results

With traditional software, there is an inordinate amount of time spent talking and reporting not about the job to be done, but about the *process* to get the job done. The reasons for this include the vast number of people involved in bringing a solution to life, the amount of time it takes, and the complexity involved. So instead of developing better software, we are forced to focus on developing "better" specification, design, and project management tools, much of which is focused on the process and not the result. It's one of those things that make us feel better about what we are doing, but in fact contribute relatively little to success. We have all this paper being generated— therefore, the resulting system must be good.

Understanding requirements

There is a basic assumption in application development methodology that we can write software more efficiently if we define exactly what the user wants first. This is the result of years of experience where finished applications turn out not to fit the user's needs, and going back to change the programs afterward was extremely hard to do. The common sense solution to this is to spend more time on defining a more precise set of requirements. This is the wrong solution for many types of applications.

We should know by now that requirements cannot be well defined before implementation. They are and remain "fuzzy," and the more you study them the fuzzier they get.

In any event, a significant part of the requirements lie in the future, and, therefore, can never be known in advance. The irony is that the more "accurate" and "precise" our system specifications are, the harder it will be to change the system tomorrow. In addition, the very act of building and implementing a system changes the requirements of the system. It is simply impossible to foresee what impact a system will have until it is up and running.

This is particularly inappropriate for the types of systems that are needed to support knowledge workers. These types of systems are ill suited to the creation of detailed specifications, because their needs can only be adequately understood through trial and discovery.

Freezing requirements

Freezing requirements is like telling the business world to stop changing (and the world to stop turning, for that matter), but our basic premise for building systems is founded upon this totally unrealistic idea. Of course, this idea was fine when we were writing accounting systems (which obviously don't change very much), but it is clearly not fine when we are writing software to address the constantly changing needs of knowledge workers.

For these types of systems, specifications are out of date the minute they are written—and so they should be if they truly mirror reality. And we penalize users for this! IT gets upset when requirements change and new circumstances arise that cause specifications to be updated. We actively discourage users from coming up with better ways to do things.

But change is exactly the point of today's world. Therefore, trying to develop systems in the traditional manner to address the needs of knowledge workers in a real-time enterprise is doomed to failure.

The elimination of experts

Back in 1984 when desktop publishing programs like Pagemaker and ReadySetGo appeared on the market, many advertising agencies employed high priced, full-time typesetters, and keyliners. These people were very much threatened by these programs and scoffed at their lack of precision in kerning (the process of reducing the spacing between certain pairs of letters to improve their appearance), the high cost of the computers themselves, and the limited availability of type output machines that would accept the Adobe Postscript files (not to mention the numerous Postscript errors that occurred).

Those companies that understood this attitude (companies like Adobe and Aldus) were smart enough to not concentrate their marketing efforts for their software to the people whose jobs these products might threaten. Instead, they targeted art directors, CFOs, CEOs, and VPs of marketing and creative directors. Apple donated thousands of computers to graphic design schools to educate the next wave of designers. A lot of keyliners and typesetters lost their jobs as desktop publishing crossed the chasm from innovator to early adopters to early majority. The smart ones took classes in this new technology and quickly landed new high-paying jobs that were very much in demand.

Of course there is still a need for professionals in the publishing industry. But think of how much can be done now by non-professionals. And do the job titles of "keyliner" or "typesetter" even exist anymore?

The lesson here is not that experts aren't needed. Rather, it's that technology reduces the learning curve, enabling non-experts to complete the same tasks with less training and experience. The ability to send a message over the telegraph once required an intermediary with significant skills. Now even grandma can send an email.

But when situational applications are built on a cloud-based platform, all of the underlying infrastructure, both hardware and software, is already in place. All that is left to do is focus on building the logic specific to the user's needs.

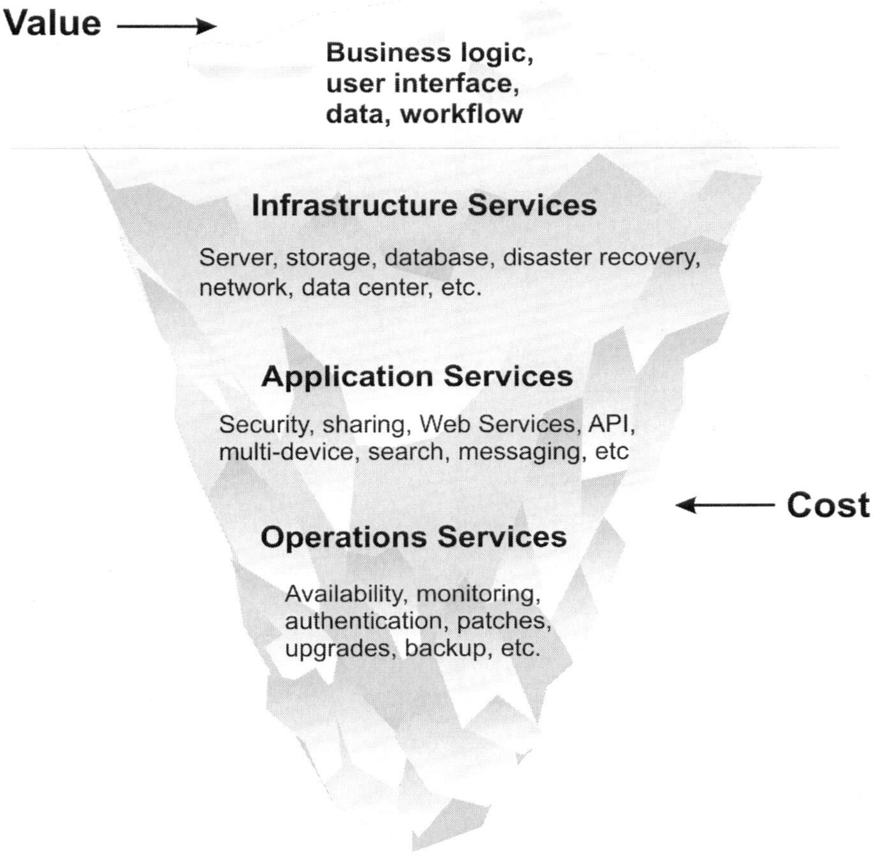

Value ⟶

**Business logic,
user interface,
data, workflow**

Infrastructure Services

Server, storage, database, disaster recovery,
network, data center, etc.

Application Services

Security, sharing, Web Services, API,
multi-device, search, messaging, etc

Operations Services

⟵ **Cost**

Availability, monitoring,
authentication, patches,
upgrades, backup, etc.

**Figure 23: The tip of the iceberg is the value to the organization that is derived from
the work of the analyst. The rest of the gang of experts
are below the surface to help make it happen.**

The following table shows how the experts (other than analysts in
some cases) are not required to build situational applications:

Figure 24: Different experts are needed to address different aspects of the application. When these aspects are part of the platform, their expertise can be eliminated.

Function	Traditional	Situational
Manage all the people involved in the project, the deadlines, communication, changes, etc.	Project Manager	Only the analyst is involved, so there is no need for a PM to coordinate and manage people.
Understand the users requirements and translate them into high-level system components.	Analyst	Analyst
Decide on appropriate technology. Translate the system requirements into a technical architecture.	Technical Architect	The technology has already been selected and the technical architecture is already built into the platform.
Write detailed specifications for the programmers.	System Designer	No programming required, so no specifications needed.
Setup a new database instance. Define the database tables.	Database Administrator	Database is already in place. Necessary tables can be defined by the analyst.

Function	Traditional	Situational
Program the application according to the specification.	Programmers	No coding needed.
Test the application according to the specifications.	Quality Assurance	Much less to test – all the underlying technology has already been tested, only the business logic needs testing – can be done by the analyst and user.
Write and update documentation	Technical writers	Platform is self-documenting.

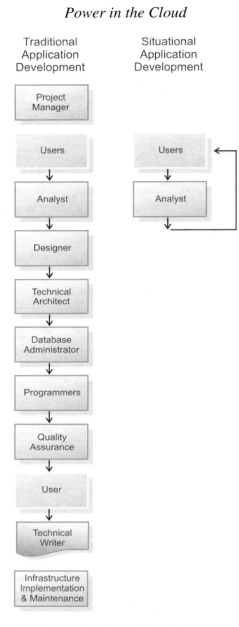

Figure 25: The number of people involved in building and delivering many software solutions is dramatically smaller.

The elimination of experts from the methodology has a major impact. The following drawing is an amusing rendition of what happens when a system is built by multiple experts:

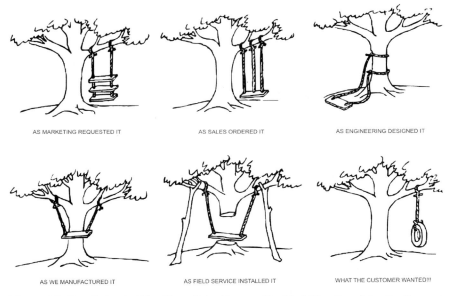

Figure 26: **Jon Pyke, in** *The Rise of the Process Enabled Situational Application* **– a Cordys** *White Paper,* **says "the above picture first appeared some 35+ years ago in a long gone publication called Computer Executive (August/September 1972 edition). It was submitted by an unknown reader to highlight the communications block between, what was then called the EDP group, and the business user. The worrying thing about this picture is that in many environments it still holds true."**

Versus traditional applications

The following is a comparison between the traditional versus situational approach to building applications:

Figure 27: The methodology for building situational applications is quite different from traditional applications. While the iterative approach to building software addresses some of these issues, the difference is that with situational applications, there is minimal actual coding involved (and everything that goes along with coding).

Methodology		
Factor	**Traditional application**	**Situational application**
Requirements definition	Requirements must be completely defined upfront, frozen, and signed off before development can start.	Because it is so easy to change the application, "freezing" requirements is unnecessary.
Feedback loop	Because the typical development team includes multiple people between the user and the person actually writing the code, the feedback between the programmer and user tends to be slow and subject to miscommunication.	The person developing the system (if it is not the user) is usually in direct contact with the user, thereby significantly shortening the feedback loop, leading to faster, more accurate development.
The impact of change	Change is the enemy of traditional applications. Requirements are frozen in time, and are only changed with great reluctance, because change creates a cascading affect across the various roles involved in the process	The implementation of changes is much simpler – there are fewer people involved in the process, and fewer components to impact (less brittle).

Methodology		
Factor	**Traditional application**	**Situational application**
Team size	A typical development team contains multiple people, and also requires a team to take responsibility for the hardware and software implementation.	Because so much of the work has already been done by the platform, it is possible to have a much smaller team work on a project. In many cases, it just takes a business analyst to build – and deploy - a complete system.
Coding standards and code walkthroughs	Because there are so many ways to program an application, it is critical that developers follow the company standard. This has to be verified using code walkthroughs.	There is usually no code, so therefore this does not apply. Everything is implemented the same way.
Maintenance	Maintenance (e.g. bug fixing) often means digging deep into code. This is especially difficult when the programmer doing the maintenance is not the same as the original coder.	Because there is no or little code, it is much easier to make changes. This also makes it easier for anyone familiar with the platform to pick up from where someone else left off.
Enhancements	Making enhancements to the code faces the same difficulties as maintenance.	Enhancements are easy to make because most enhancements are made without coding.

Methodology		
Factor	**Traditional application**	**Situational application**
Training	In most environments, each new system works somewhat differently, so users need to be trained in how to use each new system.	All the applications built on the platform work the same way, making it easy for users to learn only once.
Infrastructure procurement and implementation	Hardware, software, space, and implementation services must be procured. Software needs to be installed, patched and tested.	No procurement and implementation is necessary other than signing up for the service.
Backup procedures and disaster recovery	The application must have all these processes in place – and constantly monitor that they are in working order.	The platform provides backup and disaster recovery automatically.
Scalability	The typical application has to be built to scale across multiple servers. When more power is needed, servers must be procured, installed, etc.	The platform guarantees unlimited scalability – both increased and decreased – with no effort required.
Time to market	Given all the factors discussed above, the speed of implementation is by definition slow.	Given all the factors discussed above, the speed of implementation is significantly faster than traditional applications.

A situational methodology

The limits of end-user computing

Ideally, situational applications should be developed by the users themselves.

While this is feasible some of the time, there are many times when it's not:

- Many users are simply not interested in building their own applications.

- Even those that are interested often won't do it because they would rather spend time building their chosen career.

- There is a big gulf between users building spreadsheets and being able to write meaningful applications.

- Users who try to build their own applications may never be able to get to the aha! moment that often needs to take place when building a software solution. This may be because they are too deeply involved in their subject to be able to abstract it or they may not be capable of clearly expressing what they do – at least in clear enough terms that can be used to build an application. But the most common reason is that understanding database relationships is hard to do.

The situational application analyst

In these cases, it makes no sense to revert back to the traditional development methodology. What's needed is a methodology that takes advantage of the strengths of Situational applications and builds on them.

A solution to this problem is to create a role of Situational Application Analyst (SAA)[19]. The SAA would help translate a users requirement into system terms, model the data needed to support the application, and help translate complex business logic. The SAA could also work with IT on behalf of users to secure access to corporate data as needed.

A SAA could be a power user, an analyst, or high-level developer. But the role of SAA could become more defined in its own right as situational applications start to take hold.

Seed-Evolve-Reseed

The SAA would work with users in the following way:

---

[19] More detail on the SAA in the chapter on Implementation.

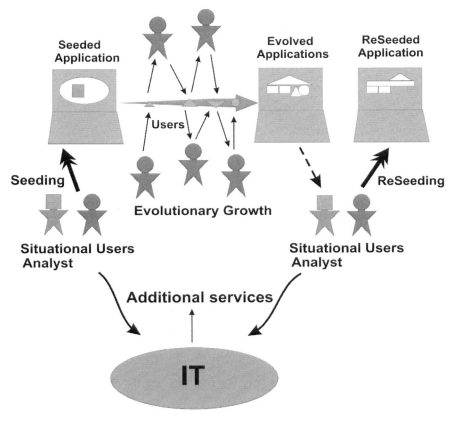

**Figure 28: The Seed-Reseed-Seed (SER) model ensures the application
gets off to a good start, and then is kept on track as it is evolved.**

- The SAA would also basically "**seed**" the application with the user. They would help the user put the first version in play.

- The user(s) would then **evolve** the application any way they like.

- There may be a point during this evolution where the SAA needs to get involved once more to "**reseed**" the application. Reseeding is necessary when evolutionary growth no longer proceeds smoothly. It is also an opportunity to organize, formalize, and generalize information and application functionality created during the evolutionary growth phase so that it can be found and shared with others. [20]

- The best solutions will ultimately emerge from these small steps forward, with the final step representing the sum total of accumulated experience"

---

[20]http://l3d.cs.colorado.edu/calendar/attachments/2008.02.13-fischer.pdf

9. The situational application platform

"Tools shape the solution. No one knew they needed a spreadsheet before Visicalc, or a home page before the World Wide Web." – Jeff Tash, Flashmap Systems, Inc.

A situational application platform provides the means to build, deploy and share software solutions.

In this section, we'll look at:

- what type of framework needs to be put in place;

- what basic functionality must be made available;

- how the platform needs to balance flexibility with ease of use.

An enabling framework

"... and likewise all parts of the system must be constructed with reference to all other parts, since, in one sense, all the parts form one machine." – Thomas Edison

A situational application platform needs a *framework* that provides a balance between the rigidity of the enterprise systems we write today and the ad hoc, one-off solutions that users employ on their desktops, like spreadsheets.

Rick Dove, chairman of Paradigm Shift International, suggests the following type of framework:[21]

> "Ten years of research indicates that a business-system structure consisting of *reusable* components *reconfigurable* in a *scalable* framework can be an effective base model for creating adaptable systems. The nature of the framework appears to be a critical factor."

To illustrate his point, Dove looks at three different types of construction toys, making observations about how they are used in practice. Construction toys offer a good metaphor because the objective of most construction toys is to facilitate the constant configuration and reconfiguration of objects – precisely the objective of the type of systems we want to build.

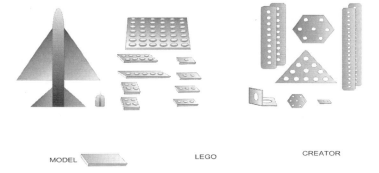

MODEL   LEGO   CREATOR

Figure 29: Rick Dove's insightful display of different types of frameworks. In the same way that complex adaptive systems exhibit vibrancy and adaptability on the edge of chaos and order, so too does a basic framework straddle the fence between too much order, where nothing much happens in response to environmental change, and too much chaos, where nothing much happens with coherency and purpose.

---

[21] Dove, Rick. *Response Ability: The Language, Structure, and Culture of the Agile Enterprise*

Erector Sets and Lego both consist of a basic set of core construction components. Both provide a framework that enables the connectivity of components into an unlimited variety of configurations. But Erector Sets are not as easy to use as Lego—Lego does not have the tedium of using nuts and bolts to connect the construction components that the Erector Set requires. This tends to inhibit, for example, the construction of large objects, and requires a higher level of motor skills than snapping together Lego blocks. As a result, Lego construction undergoes constant change. With the Erector Set kit, the first built model is likely to remain as first configured in any one-play session. Erector Set, for all its modular structure, is just not as reconfigurable in practice as Lego.

Dove goes on to contrasting these construction toys to the model-builders kit. The finished glued-construction model will have a lot more esthetic appeal than the Lego or Erector Set versions; but what it is is what it will remain for all of time. The parts are not reusable, the construction cannot be reconfigured, and one intended size precludes any scalability. A highly integrated system, this construction kit offers maximum esthetic appeal for one-time construction use. This is akin to off-the-shelf software – looks good, works well for its intended purpose, but definitely not adaptable.

In the construction-toy examples, the model-builders glued-together kit has a tight framework, a precise construction sequence, parts that are not interchangeable, and a single purpose in mind. The Erector Set, with its nuts and bolts connectivity, has a loose framework that doesn't encourage interaction among parts. It allows connections to almost anything with a hole, while simultaneously making the connection/part-interaction process tedious – often resulting in many simple constructions with novel appendages that result in chaos.

Lego walks between – each component in the Lego system carries all it needs to interact with other components, and the interaction framework rejects most unintended parts. This allows it to accommodate the moment-to-moment whim and imagination of the user with a readily adaptable system.

A Lego system is *chaordic* – it is somewhere between chaos and order, or in CAS terms, at the edge of chaos.

Situational applications call for a platform that is similarly chaordic.

Applying the analogy

These same principles can be used to create highly responsive systems and agile enterprises. Such systems and enterprises are composed of loosely coupled components whose reuse, reconfiguration, and scalability is both constrained and enabled by the framework that binds them.

To carry this analogy further, until now, the building of software has been "outsourced" to the expert builders in the IT department because it was too difficult for the lay user to understand and build their own objects.

But now, not only are people more attuned to the building process, the technology has improved significantly, so the skills needed to create meaningful objects is not as high. In addition, the need to build unique creations quickly eliminates the possibility of getting someone else to build them for you, so there is really no choice but to help people construct their own creations. The end result might not look as good as the objects created with model kits or Lego models created by the Lego company, but they work, and you can do what makes sense to you. Sure, sometimes you will want to build something so complex it takes a master Lego-builder to build it for you. And, there are some people that just love those kits and don't care that they only do what they were meant to do.

In the Lego world, each individual person can go off and develop whatever they need to develop, either alone or in groups. They can swap blocks with others, buy some from the store, or have some master builder make particularly complex construction.

The point is that at the end, every object constructed will fit with every other object made, regardless of who made it, when they made it, where they made it or what they made it with.

To make this happen, what we need is to provide a way to build better blocks and an easier way to snap them together. For this to happen, software needs to be built and delivered as a service.

Software as a "Service"

The software we use to build systems today is complicated, and its complexity rises with the complexity of the task at hand. Contrast this to Legos: using the exact same blocks and building techniques, one person can create a simple block house, while another can create a complex castle or spaceship.

We need software to be packaged in a way that can be made available to others using a standard interface – much like a Lego block.

So if I am building a situational application that requires existing data or logic, the platform should allow me to access that data or logic as a service provided to me by the platform. The complexities of how that data or logic is actually accessed, or where it is located, must be hidden. The software terms for this is "encapsulation" – a software "object" or function is encapsulated when its inner workings are hidden from the outside world – in other words, the software function is a black box. All interactions with such an object take place through its pre-defined interface (how to use the black box—what you need to send it and what it will give back, or in the case of Lego blocks, the ridges and bumps).

Encapsulation is important because it breaks up software into bite-sized chunks. Different functions can be built by different people, and as long as they agree on those interfaces, they can all work in parallel. Furthermore, encapsulated functions are defined by what they do. As long as they work as they should, nobody has to know what's going on inside.

The second ingredient is virtualization – the ability to abstract functionality to a higher level.

The first programmable digital computers dealt in the world of bits and bytes. Programs were basically a collection of zeroes and ones and output consisted of zeroes and ones. As a result, programming was very difficult and programs were quite opaque. The first step out of this black-and-white world came special programs called compilers that let programmers work with English-like languages like COBOL. The compiler could take English-like code, crunch it, and spit out the zero-and-one code that the computers actually understood. The COBOL compiler, therefore, "virtualized" the object code. COBOL statements were virtual computer commands, because the compiler had to turn them into the real commands. Humans could now work at a level of abstraction above where the computers worked.

This is the power of virtualization: the ability to layer one level of abstraction on top of another so that the tools people use get simpler as they also become more powerful.

A simple example of a software service is the following:

I am writing an application that needs to know the distance between two zip codes. I simply point to a service that provides this information. I tell it which two zip codes I am interested in, and I get the answer in my application. The service has access to whatever data and logic it needs. I see it as a highly abstracted black box.

In order for this to work, the services need to work together – like Lego blocks.

Better building blocks

Fortunately, changes have taken place on the technology front that makes this possible.

For the first time ever, the software industry actually has a real, usable, universally agreed upon open standard for creating and assembling building blocks of functionality. This new technology allows applications to be developed as a series of smaller "services" that solve immediate problems. By imposing a set of standards for the construction of any services to assure they'll play nicely with all the other services that are being developed is key to making this "on the fly" development process work.

The rules that govern this are, as dictated by CAS theory, quite simple.

XML

XML defines an open and flexible standard for storing, retrieving, publishing, and exchanging any kind of information. Firstly, it allows business information to be completely independent from proprietary data formats. This is radically different from the database chaos created by forty years of fiercely competitive attempts at differentiation on the part of database vendors.

Secondly, XML is easy to understand and use because it is written in human-intelligible language. People and machines can interpret XML information with little effort.

Web Services

Web services represent the next level of abstraction along the road to a Lego-like world for software. Encapsulating software components and applications with Web services interfaces and then virtualizing these fine-grained functional Web services into coarse-grained business services provides an opportunity to build a much more robust, powerful, and flexible IT platform.

To put the enormity of change Web services will bring in perspective, it is instructive to consider the case of the RCA jack as a simple analogy drawn to a major milestone in the development of the home electronics industry.

Before RCA's introduction of its device for connecting radio receivers with other devices, stereo systems were closed, monolithic cabinet systems.

As more manufacturers began to adopt the RCA jack, stereo components could interoperate without regard to vendor. Consumers benefited from a wealth of choices that they could simply plug in.

No longer locked into one company's solution, customers could construct a home stereo system on a "best of breed," component-by-component basis. Enthusiasts could "scale" a home entertainment system with just the right mix of equipment, and replace individual elements as budget and needs dictated. Even though, questions of scale, flexibility, and vendor lock-in for enterprise software architectures are of a different magnitude than for home stereo systems, the benefits of interchangeable components are the key to success for both models.

Web services tell the outside world what functions they perform, how they can be accessed, and what kinds of data they require. Web services do a great job of communicating with devices, people, and themselves. Their functionality is wrapped in a well-defined interface that "abstracts" the service they provide. The wrapping layer hides the intricacies of the application – the language it is written in, the platform it is running on, the database it is accessing. The only thing that matters is the interface – that is, the description of the service.

Using services with the enabling framework

Providing software a set of services that can be mixed, matched, and synchronized as needed within the context of an easily understood framework is a critical prerequisite for individuals and organizations quickly respond to changing circumstances

As we saw in the situational application example above, the best approach to building complex systems is to start small, and then to experimentally link pieces together into "chunks" until you get an effective fit. The key to this is the ability to assemble "composite applications" on the fly – applications made up of services as needed. Groups of related services can be bound together into ever-larger services. They can be strung together like a set of Christmas lights, or nested inside one another like a set of Russian dolls. In the latter case, the largest of the dolls represents what we traditionally would have thought of as "the application." But now, rather than being the entire picture, it's the sum of many smaller, interrelated pieces. Like a Rube Goldberg invention (without the complexity and wackiness), services can be assembled in a logical progression in order to accomplish a specific goal.

Of course, when you make the links, new interconnections may bring about unpredicted, emerging behaviors, which is exactly what you want.[22]

The ability to do this is the result of having a large number of small services (or situational applications) as opposed to a small number of large applications. The advantage of this approach is that the services are adaptable, evolvable, resilient, boundless, and full of potential novelty.

The other important factor is that services can be shared—between both individuals and organizations. Services are like having a whole box of Lego blocks from which many different objects can be made, knowing all the while that at any point in time, the Lego structures you have built can fit with the Lego structures of others, and they can all fit on the Lego-like platform.

The functionality required

The enabling framework facilities the provision of functionality that it needs to build applications that both make use of as well as provide services to others.

The functionality required includes the following:

---

[22] It is true of course that it can also lead to undesirable, less beneficial behaviors. But this is the price of moving forward, especially since it is often very difficult to know whether the outcome will be positive or negative beforehand. It is also true that many people dislike unpredictability. I think, however, that predictability in general is no longer on the menu. Being resilient enough to handle the unpredictable is the key to survival. This requires constant experimentation and challenges to the status quo.

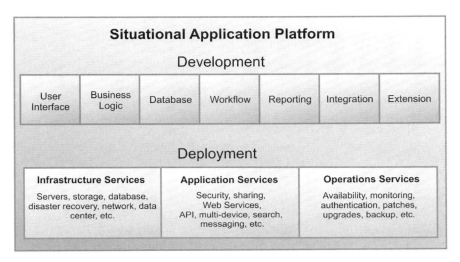

Figure 30: Every situational application platform needs the same core components.

Ideally, all functionality should be as declarative as possible – the user should always specify *what* the system should accomplish, rather than describing *how* to go about accomplishing it.

Development

Database

The user needs to be able to define and manage data without knowing anything about databases.

The most complex aspect of this is determining the relationships among entities. For example, Teachers, Students and Courses are entities. How they relate to one another can be quite complex, and how well the relationships are defined determine to a large degree how difficult the system will be to build and maintain.

Therefore, the platform needs to make it possible for the user to define these relationships using for example, a wizard approach. An alternative approach is for the system to automatically determine the database structure from a spreadsheet or forms.

Defining database relationships will often be a place where a Situational Application Analyst can play a critical role.

Other aspects of database definition must be simple to do, like defining data validation rules and default values, creating conditional database actions, and performing automatic rollups.

User Interface

The platform must allow the user to automatically generate a standard user interface from the database definition (or vice versa). More customized interfaces should be possible through the use of a visual WYSIWYG editor.

It must be possible to show data in different views, such as calendars and charts.

There should be ample control over how (and whether) fields appear on the screen. Dropdowns should be dynamic without any programming (e.g. selecting a State would then show only the Cities in that State).

Custom styling, skinning and branding should be available at the click of a button.

Business Logic

Business logic should be specifiable without writing code – either a point-and-click or visual interface should be provided. There should be extensive error checking to prevent obvious mistakes.

It should be easy to add business logic when common events occur in the system (e.g. when a record is added).

The system should automatically cater to all common actions (e.g. provide sub-totals based on groupings).

Workflow

Workflows should be specifiable without coding/scripting. Notifications should be automatically generated based on user-specified conditions. The concept of queues should be automatically supported, as should scheduled actions (e.g. check the status of this record every hour and send a notification to this person if the status is X).

Platform Extensions

It should be possible to extend the platform seamlessly - the user should not be aware that they are using a custom platform extension.

Integration

Integration functionality is critical in determining how extensively a situational application platform can be used. It includes the following areas:

External Data Sources

Data sources other than the platforms native database should be supported. The import/export of data should be available using common formats, as well as services that make data available to the user in a format that they can easily use in their applications.

Desktop Integration

There should be built-in integration with heavily used desktop software like MS Office.

Cloud Services Integration

Integration with popular cloud platforms like Google Apps, Facebook, Gmail, etc. should be available as part of the platform.

Inside-Out Integration

The platform should be able to make the functionality that is built on top of it available to external applications as services – both applications written on the same platform, as well as external applications.

Reporting

It should be possible to create standard reports using simple point-and-click. Common reporting functionality like automatic sub-totaling should be supported with little effort required by the user.

The platform should also support the ability to include external data in reports, and support multi-level grouping and multi-column formulas.

Common visualization capability like charts and maps should be available at the click of a mouse.

Deployment

All aspects of deployment should be taken care of by the platform. This includes hardware, scalability, backup, disaster recovery, performance.

The platform should include out-the-box support for things like multiple languages, multiple currencies and dynamic currency exchange rates.

Complete user management and authorization functionality should be available, including support for multiple roles and permission at a table, record and field level.

Balancing ease of use with flexibility

> Just because a user can do a database query, create a spreadsheet, or build a simple database application doesn't mean that they are capable of becoming a competent programmer. Rather, the point is that, given the right tools, they won't have to become programmers in order to achieve significant results building their own solutions. This is the challenge for situational application platform vendors.

The primary goal of a situational application platform is to empower business users who are closest to the problems being solved to quickly build full-featured collaborative business applications online, and immediately deploy those applications to the appropriate people.

A tool must be designed to appeal to the average business user. It should require no education and no programming skills, cumbersome download or installation of any new software, enabling users to focus on the problem at hand. A typical business user should be able to proceed immediately to create applications for any business task.

The best way to do this is to focus on the user's goal. As we will see later, "Goal Driven Development" (GDD) is a development process that sets the user's end goal at the center of all activities. The end goal drives the development experience and provides the abstractions and metaphors that are used through the development process; all "non goal" related details are hidden (especially technical details).

10. The situational application environment

In order to leverage the platform, effective support mechanisms must be put in place to make it as easy as possible for users to take advantage of the new tools at their disposal.

While many companies will succumb to a bottom-up, willy-nilly implementation of situational application platforms, a deliberate, step-by-step process offers the best chance of quickly leveraging situational applications across the organization.

In this chapter, we'll look at:

- How to establish a Situational Application Center (SAC).

- How to develop Situational Application Analysts (SAA).

The Situational Application Center (SAC)

Back in the late seventies and early eighties, IBM was hot on the concept of the Information Center. The idea was that there would be a group of people in IT who would look after the needs of end users by providing them with report writers, analysis tools, etc. There was even a high-level development tool called APL that was made available to power users. APL was as powerful as it was obscure – if you "got it," you could do amazing things. If you didn't, no one could teach you how to use it no matter how hard they tried. But its power was a thing of beauty. The joke was always that you could write an air traffic control system in a few lines of APL code!

I spent quite a few years implementing Information Centers and teaching APL. And for many organizations, it worked. We were able to give users solutions that they could never get from IT. We could teach users to build their own applications like econometric models in APL (the early PC spreadsheets couldn't handle the amount of data needed). This was much more effective than having them try to translate their complex requirements into specifications that then had to be programmed in Fortran.

The Information Center and APL died after I left IBM in the mid-eighties. But a new form of Information Center has started to appear from IBM, first with their Situational Applications Environment (SAC), and more recently with the IBM Mashup Center.

This concept is absolutely right for supporting situational applications. As IBM puts it:

> "The goal of a SAC is to create an ecosystem within an enterprise which would offer more autonomy to the lines of business (LOBs) by shifting some just-in-time business automation responsibilities from corporate IT to small teams and individuals."

User roles in the SAC

To stimulate a vibrant SA enterprise ecosystem, it's important to bring together users with a range of complementary skills.

Business-focused users know where business value can be quickly realized through the targeted creation of new applications. Technology-focused users understand programming concepts and data complexities.

Figure 31: **User roles in an SA-focused community**[23]

Roles	Attributes	Requirements
SA users	Business user: • Knows the business need • Needs quick answers • Has standard desktop tools	• Describe business needs for new situational applications • Demand real business benefits from situational applications • Find existing situational applications and use them • Rate situational applications and comment on them
SA builders	Business power user or LOB developer: • Understands in depth requirements e.g. spreadsheet formulae • Knows/is close to business need • Is capable of SA building	• Can access a range of tools to fit skills and domain expertise • Builds situational applications • Provide templates for Situational applications • Share Situational applications and collaborate to improve them
SA analysts	Business/Systems Analyst: • Understands how to build complex	• Can access a range of tools to fit skills and domain expertise • Builds Situational

---

[23] Adapted from *SOA meets situational applications, Part 2: Building the IBM Situational Applications Environment*
http://www.ibm.com/developerworks/webservices/library/ws-soa-situational2/

Roles	Attributes	Requirements
	databases, specify complex business rules, and define complex business processes • Is close to IT • Is capable of SA building	applications • Provide templates for Situational applications • Share Situational applications and collaborate to improve them
Service providers	LOB or IT developer: • Has traditional programming skills • Understands integration issues • Uses a range of programming tools	• Can access enterprise data • Use tools and utilities to build services • Make services available on the SA platform

The emergence of Web 2.0 social interactions means that the immense power and creativity of this corporate workforce is more accessible and connected than ever before. The SAC provides the facilities required to sustain such interaction between these user groups.

The SAC Communal Web Site

The central focus for the environment is the SAC home page. It draws the attention of users to the latest and most popular additions from the community (such as situational applications, consumables, and the latest forum threads), introduces tooling in a task-driven manner, and raises awareness of corporate guidelines for interpreting data and use of internal and external services.

The SAC Catalog

The catalog stores assets created by the community. These assets are either links to situational applications, or parts from which situational applications can be constructed. They might be Web services, JavaScript widgets, APIs, etc. - "consumables"[24].

Each catalog entry describes the asset's details and provides examples of how to use it and whom to contact about it. The details include minimal categorization augmented with tagging. Users can comment on the entry and register details of their own usage examples. They can also add tags, and both the entry and tags can be rated based on popularity and relevance. This user-generated taxonomy, or *folksonomy*, is then used to filter entries along with more traditional keyword search techniques.

Situational applications are built to be just good enough to get a particular job done. It's often not obvious to users that an application is anything other than a production-ready tool, especially to those outside the original team of interest who built it. If business decisions are to be made based on the usage of a situational application, it's important that prospective users understand the situational applications builder's original objectives.

Best practice in the SAC recommends that situational application builders provide sufficient detail in the description of their applications and include links back from the application to the SAC catalog so users can discover the provenance of the SA, rate it, and provide feedback.

---

[24] *SOA meets situational applications, Part 2: Building the IBM Situational Applications Environment*
http://www.ibm.com/developerworks/webservices/library/ws-soa-situational2/

Ideally, this capability should be integrated with the SA builder tooling so that it becomes an integral part of any SA built with that tool.

Situational Application Analyst (SAA)

The situational application analyst (SAA) has a critical role to play in the SAC.

Background

A SAA will typically have a background as a:

- Power user who is currently building situational applications in Excel and Access.

- Business analyst who is writing high-level specifications for IT.

- Soft core programmer who is writing applications in IT using languages like PHP.

Skills

The key skills a SAA must possess include:

- **Communication skills.** The SAA must be able to understand business users and work with them to help them express their needs. They must also be able to communicate with IT when there is a need for IT to provide access to data, or to extend the situational application platform.

- **Brainstorming skills.** The SAA must be able to encourage users to think creatively in order to reach innovative solutions.

- **Database skills.** The SAA must be able to help users translate their data needs into a data base model.

- **Logic skills.** The SAA must be able to help users translate their business logic needs into solid algorithms.

- **Process skills.** The SAA must be able to help users express their process needs into workflows.

- **Platform skill.** The SAA must be an expert in the situational application platform being used.

Responsibilities

The primary responsibilities of a SAA will be to:

- **Model**. Understand a business situation and help model the database and business processes needed to support it.

- **Express**. Clearly express business logic without error.

- **Teach**. Teach users how to use the platform most effectively in their jobs.

- **Seed and Reseed**. Help users build situational applications, first by ensuring the foundation of the application is sound, and later, after the application has been evolved by users, ensuring that the application remains solid and usable.

- **Specify**. Create specifications that tell a vendor, IT or consultant exactly what extensions are needed to the platform so the users can do what they need.

- **Circumvent.** Alternatively (in addition to), find ways around any limitations in the platform to meet the needs of the user without having to extend the platform.

- **Define.** Define what existing enterprise or departmental data is needed by users in order to effectively build their applications.

- **Suggest**. The SAA should suggest and help implement links and re-use among situational applications.

11. The role of IT

"The big thing [IT will] have to brace themselves for is that the functions that until now have accounted for most of their spending and most of their hiring are going to go away, such as all the administrative and maintenance jobs that were required to run complex equipment and applications on-site. This isn't going to happen overnight, but much of that is going to move out to the utility model over time. That doesn't mean IT shops won''t continue to exist and have important functions – they might have even had some more important functions – but it does mean that their traditional roles are going to change and they're going to have to get used to, I think, having a lot fewer people and probably having considerably lower budgets." – Nick Carr, author of *The Big Switch* (in *The ways cloud computing will disrupt IT*, Computerworld)

IT as facilitator

IT will gradually move from being the exclusive provider of enterprise systems to an enabler and facilitator of solutions built by self-reliant employees.[25]

The railway companies of the last century declined because they thought they were in the railway business instead of the transportation business. The importance of corporate IT departments will decline if

---

[25] Changing the corporate IT development model: tapping the power of grassroots computing – *IBM Systems Journal archive Volume 46 , Issue 4*

they think they are in the business of building and running enterprise software when in fact they need to be in the business of empowering employees to be as effective and productive as possible.

Today, the IT department is the focal point of automation in the organization because it has the sole means of production (programmers, etc.) and the sole means of delivery (the data center). But both these factors are changing.

Cloud computing eliminates IT as the sole means of delivery – and situational application platforms eliminate IT as the sole means of production.

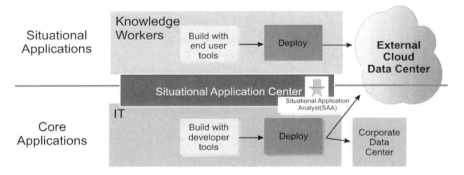

Figure 32: IT supports knowledge workers through the Situational Application Center (SAC) and interfaces with them through the Situational Application Analyst (SAA).

Organizations are reluctant to really "set people free" to build and deploy their own solutions because it is perceived as being too difficult to control what people do, and it is too difficult to harness their efforts effectively for the good of the organization. Hence, we tend to put in place structures and strictures that end up limiting employees' freedom to perform and thus contribute at the highest possible level.

But we are rapidly reaching a point where this no longer has to be the case. Information technology is now capable of providing the infrastructure that allows users the freedom to become self-reliant, but in a way that is compatible with the goals of the organizations.

Unfortunately, most companies are just not set up to handle this new way of doing systems. They are trapped in an IT-centric development process, and the thought of giving business users the ability to do things themselves seems like a big leap. But in the same way that outsourcing a spreadsheet to IT today is absurd, so too will outsourcing typical business applications in the future.

To succeed in today's world, an organization must sweep away the notion of IT as the sole provider of information systems. Employees are willing and able to take responsibility for computerizing their part of the business—within the context of an enterprise platform that facilitates reuse and sharing. The new generation is not interested in waiting for IT to get around to meeting their needs. As a result, IT will become less and less visible in solving the problems of its user base and more of a facilitator for the users to take care of themselves.

A new opportunity for IT

The demand for IT projects always exceeds ITs ability to deliver them all. IT is able to address only those most highly prioritized, core business projects that receive the budget, staff and priority to develop, test, deliver and maintain over time. If projects don't make the "A" list, the project either doesn't get done or workers have to find a way to do it themselves.

Situational applications offer new opportunities for IT to enhance its value to the organization and help the organization become more effective:

- Situational applications provide IT with capabilities outside the IT department. IT needs to harness this capability to increase the impact of IT in the organizations. Failure to embrace this means wasted resources, an inability to maximize the value of your companies collective candlepower, and lost opportunities.

- Situational applications are an opportunity for IT to service low-end, disenfranchised users.

- Situational applications are an effective way to tackle high-value back-burner issues and alleviate the IT bottleneck.

- Situational applications provide the means to improve worker effectiveness through better tools and services that enable workers to create their own specialized ad hoc applications.

- Situational applications have the potential to restore the luster of many IT departments, because these solutions are focused on delivering "customized, situational applications" that connect to a range of common and uncommon processes.

To take advantage of this opportunity, IT needs to recognize situational applications as a "good thing." IT needs to internalize that there are capabilities outside the IT department that need to be used. This is not new – it already lurks just out of sight, in Excel spreadsheets and Access databases. Failure to embrace and support this "Shadow IT" means wasted resources, an inability to maximize the value of your company's collective brainpower, and lost opportunities.

New IT Services

Situational Application Analysts

There will be an increasing need for Situational Application Analysts (SAA). The SAA will be on the front line in IT's new role as facilitator rather than provider. The SAA will foster an environment in which workers can share their solutions with others, help improve solutions through collaboration, and support the users continued building of solutions to meet new and evolving business needs.

Environment seeding

Situational applications that rely on existing data can be built much more effectively and quickly when a base inventory of enterprise feeds is pre-established so the feeds can be consumed and mixed as needed for a given application.

Creating an inventory of data feeds allows IT to focus on how the information needs to be delivered rather than how to find and enable it. Establishing an inventory of feeds is a highly cost-effective and pragmatic way for situational applications to work with legacy systems, and can go a long way toward helping satisfy unmet LOB information access needs.

Develop and unlock data

Information sources need to be unlocked and made available in a format that can be consumed by the situational application platform.

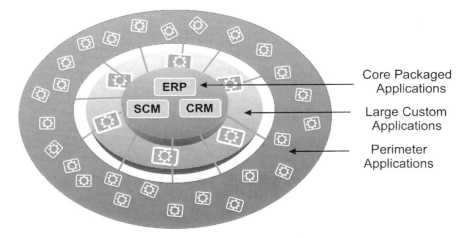

**Figure 33: IT needs to create "spokes" of data
that can be used by the perimeter applications.**

Transform data

Information sources can be mixed and mashed together to make them more useful. They can be filtered, merged, combined, grouped, sorted, annotated and augmented. New and purpose-built information feeds can be quickly and easily created for the need at hand. These operations are usually accomplished using a graphical tool that provides real-time previewing of feeds as they are created. The format of the outbound feed can also be transformed, regardless of the original information sources, into standards-based formats for consumption by the sit app platform.

Ensure data quality

When data access is opened for use in situational applications, sometimes fields that have traditionally been unimportant or even hidden are made available. Users can often assume levels of completeness and consistency that in reality do not exist. A classic example is address information that has been collected by many applications and made use of in freeform style. A situational application builder who may want to use that data for assigning an address programmatically will find that the inconsistent address information styles now need to be handled with complex logic.

Lightweight governance

Although each situational application is relatively simple, the enterprise IT environment will grow in heterogeneity and complexity. To shield users from these intricacies, the IT department can employ lightweight governance to prevent them from inadvertently damaging their own solutions or the solutions of others and to prevent the accidental disclosing of protected assets or the violating of agreements with third- party asset providers.

Power in the Cloud

12. Conclusion

"In a revolutionary era of surprise and innovation, you need to think and act like a revolutionary. (People who don't act that way have a particular name: victims)."
– Joshua Cooper Ramo, *The Age of Uncertainty*

In an era when change arrives without warning and threatens to eradicate entire companies and industries overnight, organizations can survive and prosper only by engaging the eyes, ears, minds, and emotions of all employees, providing them with the right tools and encouraging them to use their initiative to adapt the organization to the changes buffeting it.[26]

Empowering individuals and teams to take responsibility for building solutions for themselves will produce the flywheel affect— each small push, taken together over time, can have an enormous impact over time.

Imagine the level of innovation that can be achieved by enabling your employees to create applications that help them solve a situational problem or take advantage of a new business opportunity.

The benefits of many of these types of applications are intangible and difficult to quantify. But in the aggregate, they can have an enormous impact on the enterprise.

Indeed, situational applications represent billions of dollars in potential productivity gains, higher customer satisfaction, new business opportunities, faster time to market and innovation.

---

[26] *The New Pioneers,* Tom Petzinger

To realize this potential, it will not be enough to simply acquire a situational application tool and hope for the best. A tool alone will not transform an organization. It requires a concerted effort that brings together all the necessary strands of platform, methodology and mindset.

Once these are in place, you can set your employees free. The result will be a peak-performing, robust and sustainable organization – based on the shared efforts of thoroughly empowered employees.

The influx into the workforce of millions of fresh thinking, energized, adaptable, self- reliant youth, armed with the most powerful tools ever created, will make this task much easier to achieve. In any event, the increasing value of knowledge workers will force this change to take place – those that don't change will not survive.

13. How to get started

Ok, so you are convinced that this is a good thing to do. Now what?

Here are some first steps to take:

What platform should I use?

Visit the Power In The Cloud site www.PowerInTheCloud.com to look at:

- What platforms are available?

- What evaluation criteria can be used?

- What reviews have been written about the platforms?

- What issues have been reported?

- What case studies have been reported?

What applications should I start with?

- Review your backlog. You are likely to find many applications that could be addressed by a situational application background.

- Take the Situational Application Self-Evaluation at the end of the book. This will help you very quickly identify areas of your organization that could benefit from situational applications.

- Review the chapter on leveraging situational applications and match the patterns to your business. This will likely highlight potential areas that match your particular circumstances.

What should I do first?

Run a pilot

Once you have identified a platform and a first application, run a pilot. There is no upfront expense – all the platforms are free and will only start billing you when you add users and go live.

Evaluate the pilot

After the pilot has been successfully completed, evaluate its success:

- Did the application meet the challenge it was designed to address?

- What went wrong? What went right?

- Did the platform work as expected? If not, why not? Is it a problem with the platform? Is the platform a poor fit?

What do I do after the pilot?

Establish a Situational Application Center

- Put in place a web site that explains what is available and grows into a comprehensive catalog and corporate community.

- Select a business-minded developer (or IT-minded user) to become your first Situational Application Analyst to assist with the initial applications and to interface with IT.

- Alternatively, hire a knowledgeable consultant to come in to implement and support your situational application environment.

Educate your knowledge workers

Attend a Situational Application Workshop

Visit www.PowerInTheCloud.com to sign up for one of the workshops. This is an excellent way to educate your knowledge workers as to how they can leverage your new situational application environment.

Run a Situational Application Workshop In-House

Contact PowerInTheCloud, Inc. to schedule an in-house workshop to educate your knowledge workers as to how they can leverage your new situational application environment.

Roll out your Situational Application Environment

Make everyone aware of what is available, how they can get started and where they can get help.

Feeling Stuck?

If you are looking for advice on how to proceed, feel free to Email me at book@PowerInTheCloud.com.

Let me know what happens

My next book will track failures and successes in situational application implementations. I would love to hear from you. Email me at book@PowerInTheCloud.com.

14. Perspectives

I asked experts in their fields to provide their perspective on key topics related to situational application platforms:

Jeffrey Kaplan gives us his perspective on why the time is right for Software as a Service (SaaS);

Asaf Adi, Samuel Kallner and **Yoav Rubin** describe the research they have been doing at IBM in order to better understand how business users can build their own applications; and

Jon Pyke of Cordys describes why we need process enablement to provide ownership, control and auditability of situational applications.

Why the Time is Right For SaaS

By Jeffrey M. Kaplan, Managing Director, THINKstrategies

Jeff has over twenty years of experience and recognized expertise in IT/network management, SaaS, managed services, cloud computing, telecommunications and outsourcing trends. He founded THINKstrategies to address the unprecedented IT/network management and sourcing issues facing enterprise IT executives, IT solutions providers and venture capital firms today. Kaplan has a history of success working with clients from each of these sectors. Jeff also founded the SaaS Showplace and Managed Services Showplace, the leading vendor-independent online directories and best practice resource centers in these rapidly growing marketplaces. Jeff is also a senior advisor to Triple-Tree, LLC, serves as a member of the On-Demand Services steering committee of the SIIA, and is the chairman of the SaaS/cloud computing/managed services track of NetworkWorld's IT Roadmap and Interops.

The world is fundamentally changing.

Globalization and eCommerce are changing the competitive landscape. Mobility and technology are changing the nature of the workplace. And, a new generation of employees is changing the concept of workgroups. Customer loyalty is a thing of the past; as is the traditional, centralized office.

Today's intensifying economic pressures and growing uncertainties are compounding these challenges are driving businesses of all sizes to find new ways to win and retain customers, and support their employees while reducing their operating costs.

Although technology and applications were supposed to help businesses address these challenges, in many cases they have only compounded the problems facing organizations of all sizes because of their exorbitant costs and complexities.

Legacy on-premise, packaged software applications were not designed to satisfy the requirements of today's workplace. Instead, they were architected to sit behind a firewall and configured to be extremely difficult for end-users to access remotely. Legacy applications also require a significant upfront capital investment, expensive consulting services, long deployment cycles, and ongoing maintenance costs just to keep the applications up and running.

Despite these investments, the Standish Group has found *nearly a third (31.1%) of software projects have been cancelled before they are completed.* And, of those software deployment projects which have been completed, *over half (52.7%) have taken twice as long or cost twice as much as originally expected.*

AMR Research has also found that many organizations can *spend up to ten times the cost of the software license deploying and managing the application.*

Many companies are also discovering that their enterprise applications are being under-utilized by their end-users because the applications are either inflexible or not user-friendly. The inefficiencies of traditional, on-premise software can no longer be tolerated in today's tough economic environment.

As a result, a growing number of organizations are turning to a new generation of web-based, Software-as-a-Service (SaaS) solutions that offer greater functionality specifically designed to address the rapidly changing needs of today's businesses.

These cloud-based services emulate the design features and business best practices of the leading online consumer services – such as Amazon.com, Apple iTunes and YouTube—to provide the same level of flexibility and ease-of-use to the business world.

Over the past three years, THINKstrategies has seen a steady increase in customer interest and adoption of on-demand SaaS solutions. Our most recent survey of over 100 companies conducted in October 2008, in conjunction with Cutter Consortium, found 63% of the companies had adopted a SaaS solution—*nearly double the percentage in 2007!* (See, Figure 1.)

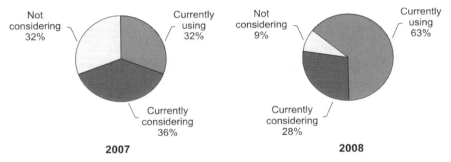

Figure 1: Percent of Companies Using and Considering SaaS Solutions
(*Source: THINKstrategies/Cutter Consortium 2008.*)

Not only are businesses adopting SaaS at a greater rate than the major market research firms recognize, but THINKstrategies and Cutter Consortium's surveys also found that over 90% of SaaS users are satisfied with their solutions, plan to expand their use of SaaS, and would encourage their peers to consider SaaS solutions. No legacy software vendors can match these figures.

It is for these reasons that IDC recently predicted the SaaS market would triple in size over the next five years. The research firm forecasts the market will experience a 24.4% compound annual growth rate (CAGR) and will exceed $15 billion in 2012, while Gartner predicts the traditional enterprise software industry will only grow 6.6% because of its poor track record.

186

Companies of all sizes are discovering that today's SaaS solutions are perfectly designed to respond to the current challenges in a more reliable and cost-effective fashion. SaaS solutions eliminate the upfront costs and ongoing risks associated with traditional, on-premise software. These solutions enable end-users to take advantage of the software functionality more quickly and easily without having to worry about the hassles of deployment and maintenance.

Despite the obvious benefits of SaaS and a broader array of cloud computing services, established software vendors are facing serious obstacles to delivering their own on-demand solutions. They lack the development skills and go-to-market strategies to successfully build and deliver these services. They also face the threat of internal cannibalization of their existing on-premise products, potential competition within their direct and indirect sales channels, and investor revolt due to the revenue recognition issues associated with 'pay-as-you-go' services.

As a consequence, the SaaS and cloud computing market represents fertile ground for start-ups and a treacherous minefield for established players. This poses a combination of opportunities and challenges for potential users of SaaS and cloud computing solutions.

While the proliferation of new players has created a "buyer's market" for users, a combination of market saturation and funding pressures brought on by today's economic crisis is setting the stage for an industry shakeout.

Therefore, IT and business decision-makers considering various SaaS and cloud computing alternatives must carefully evaluate the financial viability of the potential vendors as well as their functional capabilities.

If they make the right vendor choices, organizations of all sizes can quickly gain substantial and measurable business benefits from today's rapidly evolving SaaS and cloud computing solutions.

The Future: Goal Driven Development For Situational Applications

By Dr. Asaf Adi, Samuel Kallner and Yoav Rubin, Simplified Middleware & Tools at IBM's Haifa, Israel Research Lab

Dr. Asaf Adi – Manager of the Simplified Middleware and Tools group at the IBM Research Laboratory in Haifa, Israel. Dr. Adi received a B.Sc. and a Ph.D. from the Technion - Israel Institute of Technology. His research is focused on simplified middleware and tools, targeted at business users and business developers for next generation environments including Web 2.0, software as a service, mobile devices, virtual worlds, and cloud computing platforms.

Samuel Kallner – A member of the Simplified Middleware and tools group at the IBM Research Laboratory in Haifa, Israel. Samuel received a B.Sc. from Yeshiva College, NYC, NY, USA. His current research is focused on simplified middleware and tools, targeted at business users and business developers for next generation environments including Web 2.0, software as a service, mobile devices, virtual worlds, and cloud computing platforms.

Yoav Rubin holds a B.Sc. in Information Systems Engineering from the Computer Science faculty in the Technion, Israel Institute of Technology, and for the last nine years, he has been working as a Software engineer in IBM Haifa Research Lab, mostly in the fields of visual application development tools and complex event processing. His main interests are Java and Web 2.0 technologies, end user development and usability.

The following is a description of research undertaken by IBM Research to better understand what business users need in order to build software solutions on their own.

Introduction

Research Goal

The following is a description of research being done by IBM Research to find ways to simplify the development experience for business users by focusing on the user's needs as opposed to technology.

Target audience

The prototypical member of this study's target audience, the business user, is an educated professional (e.g., accountant, HR personnel) whose main goal is business-specific. Business users have modest computer literacy (and interest) that mostly include the web and MS Office, hence we can infer only basic computer experience that includes using a wizard to generate something new; interacting with spreadsheets, documents, and forms; and using drag and drop to rearrange items on the screen.

Desired result

A tool must be designed to appeal to the average business user. It should require no education and no programming skills, cumbersome download or installation of any new software, enabling users to focus on the problem at hand. A typical business user should be able to proceed immediately to create applications for any business task, including Human Resources, Finance, Sales or Marketing, that automate common manual processes, such as the collection and analysis of information.

Consequently, the delays encountered when a typical employee issues an application development request through an IT department are eliminated. As more business activities move online, there are more occasions to ask the IT department for help, but if you have to wait a lengthy period of time for support, or you don't have an IT department, you can save time, money and a lot of aggravation by quickly creating your own online business applications for just about anything.

Issues with current end user programming tools

There are two critical issues associated with building EUP tools:

Tools don't provide an appropriate level of abstraction above programming.

Simplified programming is an oxymoron - programming is not simple. To allow end users to build applications, it is necessary to *abstract* programming to a level that users do *not* program. This can be done either through more natural / human-readable language or by providing visualizations. The key is to balance between not enough versus too much complexity or information hiding.

But the level of abstraction offered to the users by EUP tools is still not sufficient. Most of today's EUP tools require business users to consider details such as navigation rules, database records, data validation, and formatting. These details are unrelated to the user's goal. Second, the level of functionality offered by the EUP controls is too low. Business users would rather specify an input field using the type of data that is about to be collected (e.g., a phone number) and not as simple text field input with an associated validation rule. This is especially apparent with complex input types such as address and person name that usually include several correlating input and output fields.

Tools don't provide appropriate ways to debug applications.

Debugging is part of development, but mastering debuggers and debugging techniques takes time and effort - this is something that is expected from developers, not end users. How to deal with failure frustration is a major problem in end user development tools. Usually developers are "problem solver" type people, whereas most of end users aren't – errors can cause psychological distress and may result in the user to stop using the tool when the first failure occurs and not try to dive into it in order to solve it.

Goal Driven Development (GDD)

Goal Driven Development (GDD) is a derivative of User Centered Design (UCD), and attempts to address these issues by focusing not only on the user's capabilities and knowledge, but also on the user's goal. GDD is most useful for long tail applications that would not traditionally be built because of the cost and time involved.

We define GDD as a development process that sets the user's end goal at the center of all activities. The end goal drives the development experience and provides the abstractions and metaphors that are used through the development process; all "non goal" related details are hidden (especially technical details).

The importance of GDD can be explained through the "paradox of the active user." Users are motivated to start quickly and complete their immediate task; they don't care about the system as such and don't want to invest time up front in getting established, setting up, and wading through while learning to use packages. Moreover, most business users do not care how a certain application is implemented as long as they achieve their goal with a minimum of fuss.

One conclusion that can be drawn is that within the context of business users, it is better to provide a tool that lets business users disregard details (such as application layout, page flow, validation rules, and databases) and focus instead on their goal; hence GDD.

It is therefore critical that the tool covers enough of the business user's problem space. It has been found that about one-third of planned web applications can be addressed by EUP tools with proper data storage and retrieval support[27] and another 40% can be satisfied by a set of five tailorable applications[28]. These findings lead us to believe that it is indeed possible to identify a set of high level goals that cover enough of the problem space explored by business users in their development efforts.

Realizing Goal Driven Development

IBM Application Creator for Business Users is a technology that has been developed based on the GDD principles. The following describes this technology and provides a glimpse of what can be done.

A Goal Driven Development Example

Think of the following scenario:

---

[27] Rode, J. and M. B. Rosson 2003. Programming at runtime: Requirements and paradigms for nonprogrammer web application development. Proceedings of the 2003 IEEE Symposium on Human Centric Computing Languages and Environments. Auckland, New Zealand pp. 23--30

[28] MacLean A. et al, 1990. User-Tailorable Systems: Pressing Issues with Buttons. In Proceedings of the SIGCHI conference on Human factors in computing systems. Seattle, Washington, United States, pp. 175-182

An onsite operations manager is interested in keeping track of the renovation costs. If the user wants to collect price quotes from various contractors, usually there would be a need to update a spreadsheet every time new information is gathered.

Putting this information on the Web with IBM Application Creator for Business Users allows anyone to access the data and update it, collect price quotes, analyze information or collect references – all in one central location without having to know how to program.

To enable the user to build the tracking application in a short period of time, IBM Application Creator for Business Users provides:

- An intuitive tool that allows the user to visually compose the user interface of the tracking application rapidly and easily.

- The created user interface is attractive and binds itself to a database to create a web-based form/data collection application. This tool does not aim at replacing paper forms and does not create web pages that look like them. Instead it creates an attractive web styled interface for gathering and updating data.

- The created application is fully secured – the operations manager can easily specify who can use the application and who has access to what data within the application. Therefore only authorized contractors can access the application.

- If the operations manager wants to include an approval cycle, creating such kind of business process is done using a simplified user interface that abstracts out any need to define a state machine (since non-technical people seldom think with circles, boxes and arrows). All the operation manager needs to define is what happens to the end user and following the end user's actions, thus by always keeping that end user in mind, the application itself is likely to be more usable.

- Once the price quotes are collected, the operations manager could use the extensive reporting system that enables creation of reports without the need to know SQL or anything else for that matter that is outside of the application's scope, and thus the operation manager concentrates on the goal (the report) and not on the report creation tool.

All the previously defined aspects of the application are created using goal-specific UI templates. These templates are the key to develop such an application, without knowing the underlying technology. Details such as page structure and navigation, database schema, and template-specific business logic are embedded in the template and do not manifest themselves to the business user during the development phase.

Forms are central to today's businesses and business professionals spend a great deal of their time in completing and reviewing forms.

The form application template in the technology provides the business user with a friendly, WYSIWYG, form development environment. The UI that is visible to the user is focused on the goal, in this case, the form. There is no place where the user can define submit buttons, data models, or mappings in a database. The user simply designs the fields on the set of forms that constitute the application from the end user's point of view. It is the responsibility of the form editor and the shell to deduce the required details automatically (e.g. database schema, relationships between data items, etc.).

Other templates

A workflow template aims to provide end users with an easier way to orchestrate or describe complex processing of data in a visual form.

With the workflow template, users can determine the transition between flow states by determining the next phase for each button. When focusing on a button, the user can determine what the next phase will be, by creating a new phase or choosing a pre-existing phase. For each button, on each phase, in addition to determining the next phase, the developer can also choose actions to be performed when moving to the next phase (e.g., what message will be displayed, who to notify on phase change, etc.).

A third template is for reporting. Business users can define reports without understanding SQL and are assisted by being able to view intermediate results while building the report.

Key future targets of research for GDD

GDD is a means to achieve a greater usability and an improved user experience within the designed and developed application. Therefore its ultimate goal is to reduce the mental gap between the user's idea of what they want, and what they perceive from the tool. These requirements define the main issues that still need to be researched in this field and assist in achieving the holy grail of minimized mental burden caused by the development environment. Achieving this will allow the users to focus only on understanding their needs and not in understanding the application creation tools. The set of issues includes the following targets:

Find the set of goals that can have GDD tools.

The set of goals that are currently known as "class book examples" of GDD are:

- create forms (data gathering)

- build reports (transform data into information)

- define workflow (dynamic data transformation by several entities / roles).

It is necessary to isolate more goals like this, and build tools designed to meet each specific goal.

Provide new ways to start an application.

Instead of the user creating an application from scratch, the user selects the goal they want to achieve (e.g. gather data). The user is then presented with a tool that they can use to meet their specific needs. This approach is similar to the long known template based development, but with a major difference, which is that the user doesn't browse templates to find the one they want, but states the goal they want to achieve and then uses the appropriate tool as a starting point.

Provide a means of dealing with failure.

The goal is to notify the user about problems at the right time, in the right way, with possible solutions. When a problem occurs, the user should not have to think of a solution, they should immediately be presented with ways to resolve the issue at hand.

Break GDD tools into more discrete goals.

Identify the right level of abstraction for these goals, by identifying the common problems / usages of each component needed to build a solution. For example, in form creation, a password field has generally two main usages: login or registration. The form design tool should therefore allow the user to state what exact usage is needed. This is similar to object oriented design where you need to first find the common ground of the problems in hand, and then find the right way to "configure" the common solution to solve all the problems in its domain (and in this process also find commonalities in these configurations).

This should not come at the cost of simply providing a huge set of solutions that fit any possible problem that might arise. For example, if the user's goal is to update a data column by X%, then the tool designer needs to find a way to bubble up this usage to the user in a more generic fashion, such as providing a tool that can build and execute queries on a database table, then allowing them to qualify their goal.

Conclusion

GDD is a critical concept for situational application tools. Current tools still require the user to think too much in terms of "how" to do something rather than "what" they wanted to do. For situational application tools, keeping the user focused on their goal at all times is the key determinant of success. GDD research is helping us figure out how best to do this.

Note: IBM Application Creator for Business Users is available from www.projectzero.org - a public incubator and developer community for Websphere sMash. WebSphere sMash is a powerful – but simple – development and execution environment designed to enable the rapid development of Web Applications.

Process-Centric Situational Application Platforms

By Jon Pyke, Chief Strategy Officer, Cordys

Jon Pyke has over 30 years experience in Software Engineering. He co-founded and is the Chair of the Workflow Management Coalition. He is a fellow of the British Computer Society and a Chartered Information Technology practitioner, he holds professional IT related qualifications and is an AiiM Laureate for Workflow – in 2003 Jon was awarded the Marvin Manheim award for Excellence in workflow. Jon is currently the CSO of Cordys, founder and CEO of the Process Factory (now part of Cordys). Jon recently co-authored a book covering both technical and business aspects of BPM. The book is published by Cambridge University Press and is called – *Mastering your Organization's Processes*.

The economic turmoil, globalization and the changes in the New World Order means that organizations cannot afford to waste time, human and financial resources on processes that can rapidly and easily be automated and managed. Businesses need to transform themselves into agile operations capable of turning a constantly changing business environment into opportunities. Process innovation and speed of change are the key opportunities for competitive differentiation moving forwards. Traditional IT solutions are finding themselves under stress as they struggle to meet the demands of the business leaders and customers they serve.

Unfortunately the IT organization, responsible for facilitating changes demanded by the business, often falls short of being able to do just that. Many studies and surveys show that changes to IT infrastructure and applications are fraught with complexity, costing much more and taking much longer than initially anticipated. It is not uncommon for an IT organization to take five or more years to make significant enterprise-wide changes; this pace just doesn't support the business initiatives required in today's business climate.

So it is inevitable the Businesses leaders are looking for new ways to use computing power to meet their needs. One of these new ways will be process centric Situational Applications.

Situational Application Provisioning

Situational Application Provisioning is a very different proposition from what we think of as applications. It therefore represents a very different opportunity and is a mechanism whereby a user can put together an "application" based around normal working patterns, using readily available services.

This means that is possible to handle any sort of business problem usually tackled by enterprise solutions by being able to leverage the capability to associate virtually any number of web services within the context of an application. Process Provisioning is effectively an application generator within a process and is inherently more flexible, easier to provide, easier to manage and easier to use than traditional "ERP" type products.

Why is This Approach Different?

Most software companies think on-demand applications (SaaS) are a replacement for traditional business software.

They couldn't be more wrong.

Sure, these Software-as-a-Service (SaaS) applications are sold as a service and paid for per-transaction, but they are developed, sold and delivered in the same manner as traditional licensed software.

The most successful SaaS companies do not think of themselves as software companies selling software on-demand, but as Web companies with business users accessing a service over the Internet. These companies realize that to effectively start and grow a SaaS business, they need to act more like a consumer-based Web company than a traditional enterprise software company.

Why Do We Need Process Technology to Deliver Situational Applications?

There are two clear reasons for needing process technology to underpin the provision of these applications:

Rapid Innovation – Ra-In Clouds[29]

The cloud is the ideal mechanism for utilizing extensive computing power – be that storage or specific applications such as SalesForce.com. As it stands it saves you money. It doesn't help you innovate – the cloud does not enable you to simply build applications to meet the needs – process technology, in its broadest sense, lets you do this in an easy and flexible way – the processes orchestrate the interaction and integration of services.

Compliance

Situational Applications can be very disruptive and can lead to anarchy and a breakdown of corporate governance and compliance. Think of all those Excel spreadsheets – Situational Applications – that are used to run most businesses – no control, no compliance, no ownership.

---

[29] Term coined by Capgemini

Process enablement of these types of applications will provide ownership, control and auditability – making them compliant with the corporate demands without stifling innovation and change.

The Application Target

The initial thrust for the cloud is data center and "standard" applications such as SalesForce.com and Google Apps. But this is just the start – the cloud has significantly more potential than simply being able to provide specialized applications and flexible data storage.

Gartner defines cloud computing as a style of computing where massively scalable IT-related capabilities are provided "as a service" using Internet technologies to multiple external customers. "During the past 15 years, a continuing trend toward IT industrialization has grown in popularity as IT services delivered via hardware, software and people are becoming repeatable and usable by a wide range of customers and service providers," said Daryl Plummer, managing vice president and Gartner Fellow. "This is due, in part to the commoditization and standardization of technologies, in part to virtualization and the rise of service-oriented software architectures, and most importantly, to the dramatic growth in popularity of the Internet."

Plummer said that taken together, these three major trends constitute the basis of a discontinuity that will create a new opportunity to shape the relationship between those who use IT services and those who sell them.

As we have seen, Business Process management has a key role in enabling the cloud to deliver applications – more importantly situational applications, in a new, flexible and cost effective way – and we call this Application Service Provisioning. The cloud then has the potential radically change the way the small to medium sized business market operates and at the same time disrupt the enterprise software market making it redundant and obsolete – almost overnight.

Power in the Cloud

The author's background: a situational application perspective

Situational applications go back a long time. My own career traces the history of where we have come from and gives an idea of where things are heading.

IBM Assembler: It all starts here

I think there are two types of business application developers: those that revel in the joy of coding, and those that just want to get the job done. I am of the latter ilk. I have spent a good deal of my long IT career trying to build systems with as little code as possible. It must be because I began my IT career writing Assembly Language programs on a very old IBM 360 mainframe. Core dumps, card punch machines and a whole 8MB (!) of memory at your disposal. You really had to know how to program in those days - and it took forever to get anything meaningful accomplished.

APL: Worlds first situational application platform

When I joined IBM South Africa a few years later, I quickly discovered the joys of APL - A Programming Language. The jump from using assembly language to APL was like going from a horse cart to a space shuttle. APL was one of those phenomenal inventions that had huge potential but absolutely no mainstream appeal (see keyboard - each symbol represented some serious functionality, and stringing together a few of these symbols resulted in powerful applications). Because you either got it or you didn't (and it didn't matter how smart you were either). There was no way to get people to "get it" – I know, because my team tried really hard to make it happen!

But APL was the very first cloud-based situational application platform. It ran on an IBM mainframe, the equivalent of today's cloud. It was used primarily by business users, not professional programmers. And you could crank out applications incredibly quickly (assuming you "got it"). One Internet dictionary of programming languages describes APL thus: "Famous for its enormous character set, and for being able to write whole accounting packages or air traffic control systems with a few incomprehensible key strokes."

Information Center: Worlds first Situational Application support environment

IBM used APL extensively internally. I built a complete APL budgeting system before going on to help bank clients build econometric modeling systems in APL. IBM sought to translate its internal success with APL to its clients through the medium of the Information Center. The Information Center was designed to be a way to support end users in their use of APL and APL extensions (which happened to include a pretty good report writer). There were some successes, but when PCs came along with spreadsheets, the enthusiasm for APL died down.

But the idea of an Information Center to support the needs of end users makes lots of sense in the age of situational application platforms, and I think we will see a revival of this idea in the very near future. IBM has already started down this path with its Situational Application Environment (SAE) and IBM Mashup Center.

Magic Software: A Situational Application tool for analysts

After coming to the USA in the mid '80's, I started a consulting firm that specialized in customizing accounting systems. We made extensive use of Magic Software, which was one of the few tools that worked well with Btrieve (many of the accounting packages used Btrieve in the '90's). In its early incarnation, Magic was the perfect situational application tool – you didn't need to be a programmer to use it (and in fact many of my best Magic "programmers" were analysts), and you could crank out applications incredibly quickly. (Unfortunately, about half way through the '90's Magic lost its way as a situational application tool and moved into the professional developers camp).

Igniting the Phoenix: The advent of 21st century Situational Application platforms

In 2003, I wrote a book, *"Igniting the Phoenix: A New Vision for IT,"* which discussed mashups, situational application builders and social networks (though the terminology didn't exist yet). Rod Smith, IBM Fellow and IBM Vice President of Emerging Technologies, was the biggest fan of the book, and he wrote:

> "I'm a avid follower of Jonathan's thoughts and body of work. When starting down the current path of Web 2.0 three years ago, Jonathan's book & interviews captured exactly what is now transpiring in terms of business transformation. I have quoted Jonathan on many, many occasions; his insights into understanding emerging key business issues both from the IT perspective and the line-of-business have been truly

visionary. How much so? I've based my current emerging technology efforts around the principles Jonathan laid out - and glad I did!"

Indeed, Rod's QEDwiki tool (now IBM Lotus Mashups) contains some of the ideas expressed in the book. QEDwiki was just the start of what has become a veritable flood of situational application platforms.

(Also see book reference in *"The role of IT in situational applications," IBM Systems Journal archive Volume 46 , Issue 4*).

SnapXT: An unfortunate foray into product development

Starting in 2003, I spent a lot of time attempting to build my own version of a situational application product based on the ideas in the book – SnapXT. The Zapthink analyst firm described it thusly:

> "To bring business value to the nascent mashup market, SnapXT offers users the ability to create enterprise-quality mashups that assemble diverse IT assets and data sources in a flexible, declarative fashion. What makes SnapXT different is its multiple interface metaphors that simplify application creation and empower the users of those applications. As a result, SnapXT is pioneering enterprise mashups through their tool that offers true business value to companies looking to build Service-Oriented Business Applications."

Way too ahead of its time, not enough runway, and not enough personal experience developing a product and taking it to market killed SnapXT.

Coghead: Great potential, unfortunate ending

I started a new company, SilverTree Systems, and began working very closely with one of the most promising of these situational application platforms - Coghead. We became responsible for building part of the Coghead platform, and needless to say, I believed Coghead had huge potential before it was acquired by SAP. It will be interesting to see what SAP does with it.

Power in the Cloud: A new resource is born

As my company started casting about for a new platform that we could work with, it became obvious that there were a lot of contenders. It also became apparent that there was a lot of interest in situational application platforms in general, and it appeared that this whole market segment was starting to take off. I therefore decided to leverage my background and expertise in this area and created a Resource Center that will hopefully save people a lot of time and effort.

The Goal: An increasingly valuable resource for organizations implementing situational applications

The goal now is to grow the site as situational application platforms find their way into more and more organizations. A number of experts in the field have generously donated their time to this site, and it is my intention to continue to involve as many people as possible, with the goal being to build a formidable body of knowledge around this subject for the use of anyone who needs it.

The Great Recession: Situational Applications can help!

The unfortunate economic climate we find ourselves in will undoubtedly hasten the adoption of situational application platforms. It is much more likely that organizations will be forced to look for new ways to get things done in this environment. The good news is that situational application platforms offer a great way forward. Adopted correctly, they could mean the difference between surviving and dying, or thriving and merely surviving.

In futurologist Adjiedj Bakas' new book, ***Beyond the Crisis: The Future of Capitalism***,[30] he quotes a telling Chinese definition, "The Chinese phrase for crisis consists of two words *danger* and *opportunity*." Or in today's context, as President Obama's chief-of-staff Rahm Emanuel would have it:

> *"You never want a serious crisis to go to waste. And what I mean by that is an opportunity to do things you think you could not do before."*

During the current crisis we finally say goodbye to the 20th century and transit into a new, post-material economy, with new economic and technology pillars in the "cloud." This transition period offers tremendous opportunities!

---

[30] Bakas, Adjiedj, *Beyond the Crisis: The Future of Capitalism*, Meghan-Kiffer Press, 2009. www.mkpress.com/cloud

Further Reading

Also check out many additional books, blogs posts, references and articles at www.PowerInTheCloud.com.

Bakas, Adjiedj, *Beyond the Crisis: The Future of Capitalism*, Meghan-Kiffer Press, 2009.

Berridge, Eric and Kervin, Michael. *IT.ER.ATE or Die, Agile Consulting for 21st Century Business Success*, AuthorHouse 2008

Bonabeau, Eric. *Swarm Intelligence: From Natural to Artificial Systems*. Oxford University Press, 1999.

Brown, John Seely, and John Hagel. "IT Does Matter." *Perspectives*. 15 May 2003. <johnhagel.com>.

Carr, Nicholas. *The Big Switch, Rewiring the World, From Edison to Google*, W.W. Norton & Company, 2008

Dove, Rick. *Response Ability—The Language, Structure, and Culture of the Agile Enterprise*. John Wiley & Sons, 2001.

Enriquez, Juan. *As the Future Catches You. How Genomics & Other Forces are Changing Your Life, Work, Health & Wealth*. Crown Business, 2001.

Fingar, Peter, and Howard Smith. *Business Process Management: The Third Wave*. Meghan-Kiffer, 2003.

Fingar, Peter. *Extreme Competition: Innovation and the Great 21st Century Business Reformation*. Meghan-Kiffer Press, 2009

Fingar, Peter. *Dot.Cloud, The 21ˢᵗ Century Business Platform,* Meghan-Kiffer Press, 2009

Gladwell, Malcolm. *The Tipping Point: How Little Things Can Make a Big Difference*. Little, Brown and Company, 2000.

Hagel, John. *Out of the Box*. Harvard Business School Press, 2002.

Hock, Dee. *Birth of the Chaordic Age*. Berrett-Koehler Publishers, Inc., 1999.

Hugos, Michael, *The Greatest Innovation Since the Assembly Line: Powerful Strategies for Business Agility*, Meghan-Kiffer Press, 2008.

Kelly, Eamonn, and Leyden, Peter. *What's Next? Exploring the New Terrain for Business*. Global Business Network, 2002.

Maslow, Abraham H. *Maslow on Management*. John Wiley and Sons, 1998.

Mulholland, Andy, Thomas, Chris S., Kurchina, Paul and Woods, Dan. *Mashup Corporations, The End of Business as Usual*, Evolved Technologist Press, 2006

Pascale, Richard. *Surfing the Edge of Chaos: The Laws of Nature and the New Laws of Business*. Crown Business, 2000.

Pascale, Richard. *How Business is a Lot Like Life*. FastCompany, April, 2001.

Ramo, Joshua Cooper. *The Age of the Unthinkable, Why the New World Disorder Constantly Surprises Us and What We Can Do About It*, Little, Brown & Company, 2009

Sapir, Jonathan. *Igniting the Phoenix: A New Vision for IT*, Xlibris, 2003.

Schoemaker, Paul J. *Profiting from Uncertainty: Strategies for Succeeding No Matter What the Future Brings.* The Free Press, 2002.

Stewart, Thomas. *Intellectual Capital: The New Wealth of Nations.* Currency/Doubleday, 1997.

Tapscott, Don. *Growing Up Digital: The Rise of the Net Generation.* McGraw-Hill, 1998.

Wheatley, Margaret & Kellner-Rogers, Myron. "Bringing Life to Organizational Change." *Journal of Strategic Performance Measurement*, April/May 1998.

Power in the Cloud

Glossary

Cloud computing. There are many definitions of cloud computing, but in this book it refers to the availability of computing power "on demand" – much like electricity is available as needed from the electrical grid. In the same way that a consumer plugs an appliance into a power socket, the user opens a browser and taps into as much computing power as they need, when they need it.

Complex Adaptive System (CAS). A complex adaptive system (CAS) is a system of semi-autonomous agents who have the freedom to act according to a set of simple rules in order to maximize a specific goal. A CAS is highly adaptive, self-organizing, interrelated, interdependent, interconnected entity that behaves as a unified whole. It learns from experience and adjusts (not just reacts) to changes in the environment.

Complex adaptive systems are all around us—the weather, the ant colonies, the stock market, our immune systems, the neighborhoods, the governments, the sporting events, and, most important, the organizations in which we work. The "participants" in every system exist and behave in total ignorance of the concept but that does not impede their contribution to the system. And every individual agent of a CAS is itself a CAS: a tree for example is a CAS within a larger CAS (a forest) which is a CAS in a still larger CAS (an ecosystem).

Edge of Chaos. The phrase "edge of chaos" was coined by computer scientist Christopher Langton in 1990. It is a condition, not a location, and the edge is not the abyss. Moving to the edge of chaos creates upheaval but not dissolution. In this book, it's the sweet spot for productive change between fixed centralized control and random, decentralized anarchy.

Mashups. Mashups combine information and capabilities from more than one source to deliver new functions and insights. Mashups can remix information from inside and outside the enterprise to solve situational problems quickly. They are created by "mashing" together multiple information sources into a lightweight Web application that is "good enough" to solve a situational problem that pops up.

Platform as a Service (PaaS). PaaS is the delivery of a computing platform as a service. It facilitates deployment of applications without the cost and complexity of buying and managing the underlying hardware and software layers, providing all of the facilities required to support the complete life cycle of building and delivering web applications and services entirely available from the Internet - with no software downloads or installation for developers, IT managers or end-users. (Wikipedia)

Situational applications. The term "situational application" has come to represent an alternate approach to building and deploying "good enough" software solutions for specific situations. Situation applications are typically built for just a handful of users, used for a relatively short period of time, or address just a small piece of functionality.

This contrasts with more common Enterprise Applications, which are designed to address a large set of business problems, require meticulous planning, and impose a sometimes-slow and often-meticulous change process. (Wikipedia)

Software as a Service (SaaS). SaaS (typically pronounced 'sass') is a model of software deployment whereby a provider licenses an application to customers for use as a service on demand.

Appendix: Self-Evaluation

"Opportunities to make money by being responsive have exploded." – Michael Hugos, *Business Agility: Sustainable Prosperity in Relentlessly Competitive World*

The following is a set of questions you can ask yourself about your organization. It will highlight where to look for opportunities to build situational applications that will squeeze waste, eliminate inefficiency, accelerate the flow of information, improve and speed up decision making, integrate business processes into a seamless chain, get the right information to the right person at the right time.

Spreadsheet abuse

- Is data re-keyed into Excel spreadsheets for reporting and analysis?

- Is data captured in spreadsheets?

- Are spreadsheets frequently emailed to co-workers or clients for data collection and synthesis?

- Do spreadsheets live on a shared drive to enable multiple parties to access and update it?

- Do spreadsheets have a version or revision number?

- Have spreadsheets become part of a core process?

- Are there applications where "manual" calculations are done, e.g., entered into Excel, then answers input into a system?

Expert abuse

- Are experts being asked the same question over and over? Can the information they provide be packaged into software?

- Can expertise that exists in the organization be packaged and sold?

Customer-centric applications

- Is your web interface with your clients customized to the specific needs of each client?

- When your client interacts with your organization, do they feel that they are special to you – that you understand their needs and have catered specifically to them?

- Even better, can they (or you) customize their interface with your organization to meet their needs?

Data collection and validation

- Is data thoroughly validated when it is entered into the system the first time?

- Is the same data entered into the system (or multiple systems) more than once?

- Do people who could enter data themselves instead communicate their information to others who then enter it for them?

Customer self-service

- Can your customers do the following without interacting with your employees:

    o Get an estimate for potential services or products?

    o Place their own orders?

    o Check their order status?

    o Check their invoice status?

- Are your employees asking customers for information that they should be able to pull up from your systems?

- Are your employees asking customers for information that the customers themselves could enter over the web?

- Do you have an easy way for your clients to submit ideas to your organization on how you can better serve them?

- Do you automatically send out questions and follow-ups to your clients to get continuous feedback?

Vendor/Partner self-service

- Are vendors able to get the answers they need from your organization by themselves?

- Are your employees asking vendors for information that the vendors themselves could enter over the web?

Information availability

- Is enterprise and silo-ed line of business data easily available to those who could use it?

- Is this data available in a form that makes it easy for users to build applications, create mashups or receive feeds?

- Does completing a single task require bringing together information from multiple sources?

- Does a user need access to more than one system in order to complete a single task?

Business Processes

- Are there tasks that are performed over and over that can be automated?

- Is work passed around efficiently between different people and systems?

- Are requests automatically routed to the most appropriate person?

- Are there delays when users are unaware they can move forward with a process?

- Do tasks get done late or not at all because they are not easily visible?

- Are people automatically reminded to complete a task when it becomes overdue?

- Does management have insight into the status of critical tasks for business, auditing or regulatory needs?

- Is key information stuck in workers' inboxes?

- Are processes repeatable, traceable and open to analysis?

- Are employees sometimes working with out-of-date information?

- Are there long e-mail chains that cover a single request, problem or activity?

- Are employees being blindsided by critical tasks that fall through the cracks?

- Are there areas of the organization where deadlines are being missed?

- Is it possible for stakeholders to find the information they need by accessing it themselves, e.g., no need to hunt other people down or comb through emails to find out the status of a work request?

- Could status meetings be eliminated if the status were readily available through a system at all times?

- Are requests and information flow to coordinate business activities between different people and systems done through email, spreadsheets, and ad-hoc manual processes?

Information accessibility

- Is enterprise data available as feeds and widgets in order to make it easily accessible by employees, clients and partners?

- Can your customers quickly find the most accurate, up-to-date information about what you are offering?

- Can users aggregate the pieces of information they need, in the format they need it, without having to resort to spreadsheets?

- Are there data sources that could be made available to users in a form that they could use at will that would have an immediate impact?

- Do employees need to access multiple applications at once in order to complete a single task?

Decision making

- Are decisions being made without the right information being available?

- Are decisions being made that are being based on missing or incomplete information?

- Are employees being overwhelmed by too much information, thereby impairing their ability to make the right decisions?

- Are employees being hampered by information being scattered in multiple repositories and databases all over most organizations?

Monitoring

- Do you have automatic monitors in place to notify the appropriate person when a task is late?

- Do you have monitors in place to determine when thresholds are crossed that indicate a problem? E.g. this department has been late with this type of order more than 10% of the time.

Information searching

- Are knowledge workers spending a significant part of their time searching for information that could be made more readily available?

- Do knowledge workers have a good success rate in finding the information they need to do their jobs well?

- Do knowledge workers spend time re-creating work that already exists but can't be found?

- Can knowledge workers easily find out who is working on which topic anywhere in the world and what they have written about it?

- Can knowledge workers get at e-mail exchanges that may form the basis for a decision?

— Companion Book —

DOT.CLOUD

The 21st Century
Business Platform

PETER FINGAR

The Business Implications!
www.mkpress.com/cloud